THE GLORIOUS BOOK
of
GREAT BRITISH WEAPONS

GEORGE COURTAULD

THE GLORIOUS BOOK of GREAT BRITISH WEAPONS

ILLUSTRATIONS BY MAI OSAWA

EBURY
PRESS

1 3 5 7 9 10 8 6 4 2

Published in 2008 by Ebury Press, an imprint of Ebury Publishing

A Random House Group Company

Copyright © George Courtauld 2008
Illustrations copyright © Mai Osawa 2008

George Courtauld has asserted his right to be identified as the author of this Work in accordance with the Copyright, Designs and Patents Act 1988

The Random House Group Limited Reg. No. 954009

Addresses for companies within the Random House Group can be found at
www.randomhouse.co.uk

A CIP catalogue record for this book is available from the British Library

The Random House Group Limited supports The Forest Stewardship Council (FSC), the leading international forest certification organisation. All our titles that are printed on Greenpeace approved FSC certified paper carry the FSC logo. Our paper procurement policy can be found at www.rbooks.co.uk/environment

To buy books by your favourite authors and register for offers visit www.rbooks.co.uk

Design by Estuary English
Printed and bound in China

ISBN 9780091909321

CONTENTS

INTRODUCTION

I WAS BORN in 1964, four years after National Service ended in Britain. Almost every man I knew as a child had some experience of military service. Many had fought in the Korean or Second World War – some even in the First World War – and I admired them enormously.

Dr Johnson once said that every man thinks less of himself for not having been a soldier. Certainly the courage to defend your family, your country, your values has been recognised down the ages as one of the measures of manhood.

Perhaps that is why boys are so fascinated by weapons: this association with manhood and power – the power of life and death. I have always been fascinated by weapons. My mother was a crack shot with a Beretta pistol. There is a photograph of her in a wonderful Sixties straw hat and sunglasses taking careful two-handed aim at something in the distance – far more glamorous and deadly than any Bond girl.

My father loved shooting and did his National Service with the Grenadiers. He looks incredibly dashing in a black-and-white photograph taken when he must have been no more than 19 years old – in ceremonial tunic, cradling a magnificent bearskin – and rather gentle.

It is not just the simplicity, the heft, the potency of so many weapons that fascinates – it is their symbolism and history.

Throughout the ages, weapons have made and changed history. The image of the outraged Boadicea, in her war chariot, rousing the British against tyranny and injustice, is echoed by Elizabeth I, in metal breastplate, addressing her troops at Tilbury while they await the Spanish Armada.

The ordinary English bowman standing against the thundering mass of armoured knights at Agincourt is paralleled by the British Expeditionary Force, a unit the German Kaiser dismissed as a 'contemptible little army', holding up the unstoppable German war machine at the start of the First World War with Lee Enfield Rifle fire so fast and accurate it was mistaken by the Germans for that of machine guns.

The longbow not only empowered ordinary Englishmen to bring down the flower of chivalry, the mounted French knights, it also changed English society as a whole. When the man in the street is armed with and trained in the use of something as lethal as a longbow, the high and mighty abuse him at their peril.

In theory, one would have expected Christian societies to have a problem with the use of weapons. The Ten Commandments are clear: 'Thou shalt not kill.' In Matthew's Gospel, Jesus states explicitly, 'Resist not evil: but whosoever shall smite thee on thy right cheek, turn to him the other also.'

Over the centuries, however, Christian philosophers like St Augustine of Hippo developed the theory of the 'Just War', consisting of five essential points:

- Force may only be used to correct or thwart a 'grave evil'.
- Only duly constituted public authorities may use deadly force or wage war.
- War may only be used to avert or right wrong – not for material gain.
- There must be a good chance of winning.
- War must be the last resort – all peaceful alternatives having been exhausted.

Too often, sadly, the theory of the Just War has remained just that, no more than a theory.

But however just or unjust the war, honest, honourable, compassionate men and women have considered it their duty to answer the call to arms. It is those weapons, those arms, that are the subject of this book.

I have used the term 'weapon' very loosely. The book was originally suggested by my three sons and some of their friends. When I asked them which weapons they would like included, they named guns, ships, swords, aeroplanes, regiments and even armies; everything from the SAS to the tin hat, from the Spitfire to the Tower of London. British

instruments of war might be a better title, especially those that were widely used and had a significant impact on the success or failure of our armed forces.

In researching the 'weapons' it was intriguing to learn how reluctant the fighting establishment so often was to embrace innovation, whether it was the screw propeller or the rifle, but I suppose when it comes to killing and being killed, better the devil you know.

On the other hand, it is amazing how real national emergency, all-out war, can speed up technological advance and cross-fertilisation. Inventions such as the tank, even the Sten gun, were copied almost as soon as they appeared.

It did seem to me that many of the weapons had a very British character. We are a martial nation – great warriors. We are also great poets, gardeners, pet lovers and merchant adventurers – any number of things – surely only the British could have created 'Hobart's Funnies', the Dam Busters' bouncing bomb, or the PIAT, an anti-tank shoulder mortar that required you to lie on your back and pull like mad just to cock it.

Weapons reveal much about the people who wield them. The way they live and the way they die. Despite the power and potency of our weapons, and their potential for destruction, the British armed forces have been an amazing force for good in the world. We have so much to be proud of and grateful for. Over the ages, men and women of astounding courage, determination and integrity have been numbered within their ranks. Some returned to civilian life, others did not. Their sacrifice is summed up in the words of the Kohima War Memorial to the Forgotten Army of the Second World War:

WHEN YOU GO HOME, TELL THEM OF US AND SAY
FOR YOUR TOMORROW WE GAVE OUR TODAY.

PART I

WAR CHARIOTS *to* CLAYMORES

THE WAR CHARIOT OF THE ANCIENT BRITONS

BACKGROUND

For most of us, the British war chariot immediately conjures up an image of the ancient British Queen Boadicea, bravely defying the Romans. According to the Roman historian Tacitus, she used her chariot as a platform from which to rouse her 250,000 troops before the Battle of Watling Street in AD 61, persuading the tribes that it was not only normal but lucky for the British to be led by a woman. A message that has resonated through the ages in the times of Elizabeth I, Queen Victoria, our own Queen Elizabeth II and even the Prime Minister Margaret Thatcher. The Roman historian Tacitus quoted Boadicea as saying, 'I fight not for my kingdom or for booty, but for my love of freedom, my bruised body, my outraged daughters. We will win this battle or perish! This is what I, a woman, will do. Men may live in slavery.'

The Romans had originally invaded Britain in 55 BC, under their great general Julius Caesar, to punish the Britons for supporting the Gauls in France. In his account of the campaign he mentions 4,000 chariots stalking his line of march. He returned a year later with four legions and forced the British tribes to pay tribute. Eventually, however, thwarted by the weather, guerrilla tactics and the political situation back in Rome, Caesar had to abandon his British ambitions.

The Romans did not return to Britain until, 90 years later, anxious to prove himself with new conquests, the Emperor Claudius sent an army of 40,000 men plus elephants in AD 43. The Emperor accepted the surrender of the British tribes in person and was on English soil for 15 days.

In AD 58 the Emperor Nero appointed a new governor, Suetonius Paulinus, who led his army to Anglesey to wipe out the Druids.

Perhaps prompted by this, but also by the fact that on the death of her husband, despite his cooperation with the Romans, his property was confiscated, his daughters were raped and she herself was flogged, Boadicea, queen of the Iceni in what is now Norfolk, roused her tribe in revolt. They were joined by the Trinovantes and other tribes and set about wiping the Romans off the map.

The Ancient Britons, the last great charioteers of Europe, have been credited with fostering Britons' long-standing love affair with the horse and pony. Even during the height of rationing in the Second World War, horsemeat was never an option for the British housewife.

Even in Caesar's time, the war chariot had disappeared from mainland Europe. Accordingly, the Romans had forgotten how to deal with it and found it terrifying in Britain, where it was still used to great effect. The ancient Britons were Celts whose ancestors arrived in the British Isles in a series of waves from about 800 BC onwards. They were famous horse-lovers and chariot builders, and are also credited with inventing one-piece iron wheel rims for chariot wheels and the free-hanging chariot axle.

THE WEAPON

The 13 foot (4 m) long, 6 foot (1.8 m) wide British Celtic war chariot was made of wood and basketwork, had two wheels and was drawn by two horses. It carried two men, a driver and a warrior. The British did not use a bow from the chariot but threw javelins. When the javelins had been used up, the warrior dismounted to fight on foot and the driver retired to a safe distance. The chariot could return to whisk the warrior to safety if necessary.

Caesar describes sword-wielding Celtic warriors running along the chariot pole and standing on the yoke across the horses' shoulders like circus riders. He clearly admired them.

WHAT HAPPENED

Boadicea defeated the Roman Ninth Legion and sacked Colchester, London and St Albans. Although she was finally beaten at Mancetter, in what is now the West Midlands, she herself was never taken. Boadicea and her daughters committed suicide after her final defeat and their remains allegedly lie under what is now King's Cross railway station.

With the destruction of the Druids, the defeat of Boadicea and the governorship of Agricola, the war chariot disappeared from England, although it persisted in Ireland for many years.

HADRIAN'S WALL

BACKGROUND

Hadrian's Wall marked the lines, or limit, of the Roman Empire in Britain and was the most heavily fortified border in the entire Empire. It spans the whole width of modern-day England, just south of the Scottish border, and was built between AD 122 and 130 to keep out the barbaric Pictish tribes to the north.

The Emperor Hadrian visited Britain in person. He had inherited new conquests from his predecessor Emperor Trajan but was experiencing rebellious incursions all over the Empire and lost no time in bringing the borders back in line. The construction of such an impressive mark of Roman authority was a firm indication that he meant business, both within the Empire and beyond it.

THE WEAPON

When completed in AD 130, the Wall ran 73.5 English miles (118 km, or 80 Roman miles) from Wallsend on the River Tyne to the Solway Firth. East of the River Irthing, the wall was built of stone 10 feet (3 m) wide and 16–20 feet (5–6 m) high. West of the River Irthing, the lack of suitable stone forced the Romans to use turf, and here the wall was up to 20 feet (6 m) wide, but only about 12 feet (3.6 m) high.

The Wall was built from east to west, about 5 miles (8 km) at a time, with a ditch and 80 gated 'milecastles', one every Roman mile, to house 20 or 30 troops, with stone turrets evenly spaced between.

It was the legions themselves who built the Wall, from limestone where possible, or wood and turf. The milecastles and turrets of the Second, Sixth and Twentieth Legions each have different designs, favoured by their own military engineers.

First a unit of soldiers prepared the foundations, then another group from the same legion built the wall above. The 'narrow wall', a section of the Wall west of the North Tyne River for some reason only 8 feet (2.4 m) wide, is set on previously prepared foundations for a normal 'broad wall'.

Shortly after the Wall's completion, at least 14 larger forts were built along the length of the Wall, normally where there had previously been a milecastle. These could house

This 'milecastle' housed the troops that were defending the boundaries of the new emperor's Empire.

up to 1,000 troops each. At the same time, a large wide trench, the Vallum, 20 feet (6 m) wide and 10 feet (3 m) deep, with parallel 6-foot (1.8 m) banks of earth running down either side, 20 feet (6 m) wide, was dug on the southern or Roman side of the Wall. This seems originally to have been a sunken road, as well as a defence against rebellion from the south.

The Wall was manned by 10,000 auxillary soldiers, not the elite Legions, with 2,000 cavalry quartered at either end.

WHAT HAPPENED

In AD 140, after the death of Hadrian in 138, the Emperor Antonius Pius tried to push the lines 100 miles (160 km) further north and built a second turf wall, this time half the length but more heavily fortified, from Carriden on the Forth to Kilpatrick on the Clyde. Having failed to conquer the Scottish tribes, on Antonius's death, his successor Marcus Aurelius retreated back to Hadrian's Wall in 164. Whenever the garrison was reduced and the wall came under attack, such as in 196, the auxillaries came under severe pressure.

When the Romans abandoned Britain in 409 to defend imperial frontiers nearer Rome, there were no auxillaries left to man the Wall, and it gradually fell into disrepair.

Strangely, although Hadrian's Wall is recognised by English Heritage as 'the most important monument built by the Romans in Britain', it is not named in any surviving inscriptions or literature, so we do not even know what the Romans called it.

A ROMAN LEGION

The basic unit of a Roman legion was the:

CONTUBERNIUM – 8 men

8 contubernia made a **CENTURY** – 80 men

2 centuries made a **MANIPLE** – 160 men

6 centuries made a **COHORT** – 480 men

10 cohorts, plus at least 120 horsemen and an extra cohort, made a **LEGION** (roughly 5,400 men).

Carrying at least 66 pounds (30 kg), they marched at 100 paces a minute and were armed with:

- A short stabbing sword, or **GLADIUS**
- Greaves (leg armour), or **OCREAE**
- A dagger, or **PUGIO**
- Heavy-duty sandals, or **CALIGAE**
- A heavy wooden shield, or **SCUTUM**
- A helmet, or **CASSIS**
- A javelin, or **PILUM**
- Body armour, or **LORICA**

THE SAXON SEAX

BACKGROUND

The invading Saxons, from northern Germany, actually took their very name from the knife they carried, the seax. They first landed on what was to become known as the Saxon Shore in AD 367. To counteract their raids, the Roman 'Count of the Saxon Shore' was made responsible for coastal garrisons at Brancaster in Norfolk, Burgh Castle and Walton Castle in Suffolk, Bradwell in Essex, Pevensey in Sussex, Reculver, Richborough, Dover and Lympne in Kent, and Portchester in Hampshire, all specifically established and maintained to thwart Saxon attacks and settlement.

The 'sex' in the county names of Middlesex, Essex, Sussex and Wessex, standing for the East, South, Middle and West Saxons, indicates the ultimate failure of those garrisons in repulsing the Saxons in the long term. The official shields of the counties of Middlesex and Essex still feature three seaxes.

The Roman legions finally abandoned Britain in 409, and between 450 and 750 the Angles, Saxons and Jutes, collectively known as the Anglo-Saxons, settled in what is now England, creating the seven kingdoms of Northumbria, Mercia, Wessex, Essex, Sussex, Kent and East Anglia.

THE WEAPON

The seax was both a weapon and a tool. A strong, single-edged knife, broad and heavy, it was between 3 and 30 inches (75 – 760 mm) long and had a thick reverse 'top' to the blade and an angled back sloping towards the point.

Those between 3 and 14 inches (75-355 mm) long were known as 'hadseaxes'. Those over 22 inches (560 mm) long, effectively swords, were called 'langseaxes' and were primarily

The Seax was more than just a rather basic weapon and tool; it identified the wearer as a freeborn Saxon.

weapons. Finer blades were inlaid with precious wire, gold, silver, copper and bronze, beaten into grooves cut into the blade. A spike continuing back from the base of the iron blade penetrated right through the simple wood, bone or antler grip, and was bent over at the end. The grips rarely included any kind of guard or pommel.

The sheath of folded leather with a belt loop was sown or riveted down the top where the thick, blunt edge of the blade would rest.

WHAT HAPPENED

From marks found on the blunt edge of the many seaxes still in existence, it is obvious that the blunt edge of the blade was often used as a hammer, while the sharp edge was ideal for hacking, both wood or flesh, and the point for stabbing.

The seax, however, appears to have been more than just a tool or weapon. Only Saxon freemen had the right to bear arms, and it seems that wearing a seax in a horizontal sheath at the front of the belt may have been an essential badge of Saxon identity.

From the state of seaxes unearthed in archaeological digs, often reduced by decades of repeated sharpening to slender slivers no thicker than a hacksaw blade, these emblems of manhood and status were handed down from father to son and retained by their proud warrior owners until virtually unusable.

The English kings Alfred the Great, Edward the Elder, Athelstan, Edmund, Edred, Edwig the Fair, Edgar the Peaceful, Edward the Martyr, Ethelred the Unready and Edmund Ironside, who reigned between 871 and 1016, were all Saxon kings, as were Edward the Confessor and Harold II. The Saxon concepts of civic responsibility, the function of the Law, including trial by jury, and the obligation of the Crown to listen to recognised advisers, still influence Britain, and the world, today.

THE KING'S SHIPS OF ALFRED THE GREAT

BACKGROUND

Alfred the Saxon became King of the West Saxons, or Wessex, on the death of his brother in 871. The Saxons themselves had begun to invade the British Isles from what is now northern Germany 500 years earlier and had established kingdoms all over England. From 793 their English kingdoms were themselves subject to attack by savage sea-roving pagans from Denmark, Sweden and Norway, with a passion for war-making, which they called Viking, and a culture intimately bound up with the sea.

The Vikings had perfected the clinker-built longship, which they called a *snekkjas* or snakeship, after the snake's head that decorated the stern. In these vessels, which were equipped with both oars and a single large sail, the Vikings travelled to India, Russia and even North America in search of treasure, slaves and land; they conquered Normandy, sacked Paris and settled in Iceland, the Faroe Isles and Greenland, and they occupied the north and north-east of England. Being pagans, they took a particular delight in sacking and despoiling churches, abbeys and monasteries. It seemed at one point that they must overrun the entire British Isles.

Alfred, a scholar as well as a warrior, decided to challenge them on their own element – to take the fight to them at sea. He determined to build a fleet.

THE WEAPON

Alfred recognised that his fleet was to have a different function from the Viking snekkjas. His ships were not to go on long sea journeys, or follow the 'whale roads', as the Vikings put it, across the 'silver necklace of the earth', but to work together from fortified bases to which they could return to repair and refit. They could be bigger, much bigger, and accordingly taller, more stable and faster.

The snakeship unearthed from the clay in 1880 at Gokstad in Norway, where it had lain for over a thousand years, was typical of the Viking craft. It had a shallow draft for raiding up river, a single striped square wool sail, and 16 black and yellow wooden shields along

21

The Viking snake ships of Scandinavia struck terror into coastal populations as far afield as India and North America.

each bulwark, one for each of the 32 oarsmen. It was 76 feet (23 m) long, 17 feet (5 m) wide and 7 feet (2.1 m) high from keel to gunwale.

Alfred's ships were twice as long. On his visit to Rome in the 850s, Alfred had seen Mediterranean galleys in action, and he incorporated some of their best features in the ships which he designed himself. He was helped by sailors from the Frisian Islands, who were paid to man the first ships and then train his crews. Saxon warriors were expected to serve their king at sea just as on land. It seems that Alfred set up specialist teams of Saxon sailors, permanently attached to individual ships.

WHAT HAPPENED

Accordingly Alfred was the first British king to command and lead an organised national fleet into battle, a navy. His victory off the Essex coast in 885 is considered the first naval battle by an English fleet. His navy of 120 ships, all recognising the authority of a single commander, was the largest in the known world in the 9th century. It was also the seed that eventually grew into the Royal Navy and earned Alfred the suffix 'the Great' – the only British monarch yet accorded that title.

THE TOWER OF LONDON

BACKGROUND

The Vikings first appeared in Britain in 793 and, indeed, the next 200 years were a time of terrible violence and lawlessness in the whole of Western Europe. In order to see off invaders and protect their possessions and communities from random rape and pillage, local warlords began to build wooden enclosures set on top of ramparts of earth, surrounded by ditches or moats.

In the Viking Dukedom of Normandy, a special kind of castle developed, not just to guard against attack, but also to subdue the local population. This was the motte and bailey: a mound surrounded by a walled enclosure.

In 1066 William of Normandy was hoping to conquer the Saxon Kingdom of England of over two million people, with a force of just over ten thousand men.

As soon as he landed at Pevensey, William fell flat on his face – but quickly got up again with sand in his hands and the words: 'By the Splendour of God I have taken possession of my realm; the earth of England is in my two hands.' From the first moment he was scanning the horizon for a site on which to build a secure base. A week before his victory at the Battle of Hastings on 14 October 1066, he had built himself a motte. The Normans did not feel safe without a nearby motte and bailey.

The Norman castle was dominated by the motte, a heap of compressed soil at least 15–20 feet (4.5 – 6m) high, surrounded by a moat, and accessible only by a drawbridge. On top of the mound a wooden tower was constructed, and below was a bailey (or courtyard), also protected by an earthen rampart, wooden palisade and moat.

Normally thrown up in a hurry at strategic sites – bends of rivers, ports, river crossings or local high points – to dominate the immediate locality, the Norman motte and bailey castles were all built along similar lines. Between 1066 and 1165, the Normans built, or forced the Saxons to build for them, 600 castles in England and Wales. Nothing of even comparable size had been constructed on British soil since the departure of the last Roman legion in AD 409.

Over the decades the wooden towers, 'donjons' or 'keeps' were rebuilt in stone at the rate of about 10 feet (3m) a year. It has been estimated that up to one tenth of the English national budget was spent on castle building between the start of Henry II's reign in 1154 and King John's Magna Carta in 1215.

One of the first Norman castles to be built on English soil was the White Tower at the heart of the Tower of London, constructed by William the Conqueror in 1078.

THE WEAPON

The White Tower is 90 feet (27 m) high with walls 15 feet (4.6 m) thick at the base, tapering to 11 feet (3.3 m) at the top. Above the battlements are three square corner turrets. The circular turret on the north-east corner accommodated the first royal observatory.

William had the Caen stone from which the Tower is made specially imported from France and gave Gundulf, Bishop of Rochester, the great honour of overseeing the building work. Recent scientific tests have proved, however, that it is not true, as was once widely believed, that the mortar used for binding the stone together was mixed with the blood of slaughtered Saxons.

In 1194 Richard the Lionheart built a curtain wall around the Tower and dug a moat around it, fed with water from the Thames. The moat leaked terribly until Henry III hired Dutch military architects to waterproof it. He upgraded the curtain wall and used the Tower as one of his principal royal palaces. In 1240 he had the whole Tower whitewashed and it was renamed the White Tower. The Tower remained a royal residence until the time of Oliver Cromwell's Commonwealth in 1649.

In 1275 the great castle builder, Edward I, the Hammer of the Scots, built a second outer curtain wall around the old moat, which he filled in. He dug a new moat around the new wall.

The inner curtain wall has thirteen towers: the Bloody, Bell, Beauchamp, Deveraux, Flint, Bowyer, Brick, Martin, Constable, Broad Arrow, Salt, Lanthorn and Wakefield Towers. The outer curtain wall has six towers facing the River Thames: the Byword, St Thomas's, Cradle, Develin, Middle and Well Towers. On the north face of the outer wall are three bastions.

The water entrance to the Tower, through which those accused of treason, such as Sir Walter Raleigh, Anne Boleyn and Sir Thomas More, were escorted to imprisonment, is known as Traitor's Gate.

WHAT HAPPENED

Over the ages the Tower has fulfilled many functions: as fortress, palace, prison, armoury,

Despite its place at the very heart of British history, the Tower of London has never been successfully besieged.

treasury, zoo, royal mint, public records office, observatory and, since 1303, resting place for the Crown Jewels.

King John established a collection of animals at the Tower in 1204. In 1750 admission to see the lions cost 3½ pence – or the gift of a cat or dog to feed to the lions. The date of the skull of a lion believed to have died in the Tower in 1280 was verified by carbon dating in 1998. William Blake was inspired to write his poem, 'The Tyger', after a visit in 1791.

There have been ravens at the Tower since records began and legend has it that should they leave, the White Tower, the Monarchy and the Kingdom will all fall. During the Blitz in the Second World War, all but one raven died of shock. An expert ornithologist was appointed to assist the Yeoman Ravenmaster in keeping the sole surviving raven, 'Grip', alive until a new set of ravens could be introduced. Jim Crow, the oldest raven ever to serve at the Tower, died at the age of 44.

The Tower, which was never attacked, is still staffed by Yeoman Wardens known as Beefeaters, who also guard the Crown Jewels.

The Tower has held many high-ranking prisoners, the first being the Bishop of Durham, imprisoned for extortion in 1100. His chaplain brought him a casket of wine containing a length of rope, and they escaped over the walls.

Anne Boleyn and Lady Jane Grey were not so lucky, both being executed there. The ghost of Anne Boleyn is still said to walk the Tower with her head under her arm – affectionately known as the 'silent woman'.

Kings of England, Scotland and France have been imprisoned in the Tower at various times, as well as the deputy head of the German Nazi party, Rudolf Hess. The last two prisoners to be held there were the Kray twins Ronnie and Reggie in 1952 – for failing to report for National Service.

THE LONGBOW

BACKGROUND

The simple short bow seems to have been invented by primitive societies as early as 12,000 years ago, first for hunting and then for war. In due course ancient armies like those of the Babylonians, Egyptians and Persians were all equipped with bows.

The various waves of immigrants into the British Isles – the Celts, Romans, Saxons, Vikings and Normans – also bought bows but these were short bows, no more than 4 feet (1.2 m) long, relying on the springiness of a simple strung piece of wood, with a pull of up to 40 pounds (18.16 kg).

The Welsh or English longbow, the use of which was first recorded around AD 1150, is three times more powerful.

The longbow's precise evolution in southern Wales is unclear but the presumably accidental discovery of the devastating power of elm sapwood and heartwood in the right combination was quickly exploited across England. It had a profound impact on the history of Britain and Europe and indeed on English society as a whole.

THE WEAPON

It could take up to four years to make a longbow. The single piece of wood, normally yew,

often imported from Spain or Italy, would be allowed to dry for up to two years and then carefully worked into shape. The bows had a D-shaped cross-section: the flat front, which faced the enemy, was made of sapwood, while the rounded back was made of heart wood, and it was the two different types of wood working against each other that provided the unique power. The strings were made of flax or hemp, sometimes silk, and fitted to the bow by horn 'nocks'.

The yew longbow, about 6 feet (1.8 m) in length, and its cloth-yard arrows, 31 inches (0.78 m) long, with a chisel or 'bodkin' head, could kill a man at up to 250 yards (230 m). Shooting 10 aimed arrows a minute, often up to 20 a minute, to form the famous 'cloud of arrows', massed medieval British archers could stop an army of armoured knights quite literally dead.

The 5,000 English archers at Agincourt were collectively firing 700 arrows a second. It was said that the white feathered shafts protruding from the heaps of dead gave the impression afterwards of a blanket of snow.

An English longbowman was presumed to be able to hit a target the size of a man at 180 yards (165 m), though real accuracy was confined to less than half that. A densely packed mob of charging knights was unmissable.

Before battle, each archer was normally equipped with 72 arrows stuck point down in the ground at his right foot, which he would loose off in between three and five minutes, the supply constantly replaced by attendant boys. The dirt from the filthy battlefield mud often caused deadly infection to those who survived the original strike, and arrowheads were glued on to the shaft in such a way as to ensure the head remained inside the stricken victim if the shaft was drawn out, which also encouraged life-threatening infections.

The longbow was much faster and more accurate than

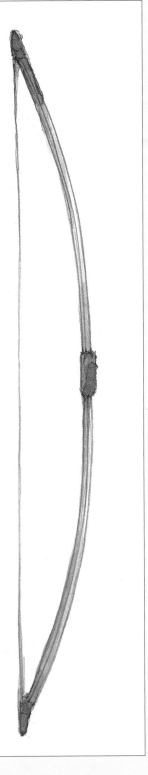

More accurate, more powerful and up to six times faster than a musket, the longbow was still to have its champions on the eve of Waterloo in 1815, but the level of training and practice required for its effective use had by then made it impractical.

either contemporary crossbows or muskets. However, the level of training required to master the weapon and cope with the 80–180-pound (36–82-kg) pull was extortionate, and few monarchies outside England had the will, cooperation or control to impose the necessary training programme.

Edward I, who conquered Wales in 1282–3, where his troops were at the receiving end of the deadly longbow, banned all sports but archery on Sundays to encourage practice. In 1363 Edward III further encouraged the use of the longbow.

Such relentless archery came at a cost. The skeletons of dead longbowmen have grossly enlarged left arms and shoulders and deformed fingers on their right hands.

Armed only with their bows, short swords and mauls (large hammers for dealing with dismounted knights), the archers needed to prepare their position carefully before battle was joined. Unready and exposed longbowmen could be wiped out by charging cavalry, so archers often carried sharpened wooden stakes which were stuck into the ground as a defence against horsemen. Alternatively, they were positioned behind natural obstacles. At Agincourt the archers were behind a stretch of marsh.

WHAT HAPPENED

During the Hundred Years War (1337–1453) between the English and French, and the Wars of the Roses (1455–87), fought between the Lancastrians and Yorkists for the English crown, the longbow dominated.

English victories at this time – Crécy (1346), Poitiers (1356) and Agincourt (1415) – were effectively won by the longbow, and the Battle of Towton in 1461, in which the Yorkist bowmen routed the Lancastrian bowmen, still remains the most deadly engagement ever fought on British soil. Terrible weather allowed the two sets of archers to get very close to each other, and 20,000 were killed.

Although the last recorded use of the longbow in combat was at Bridgnorth at the outbreak of the Civil War in 1642, the weapon had a lasting impact. The longbow victories strengthened England's belief in itself as a land set apart, with a special invulnerability and destiny, and uniquely valiant and ferocious ordinary men and women. The legend of Robin Hood, the notion of the insulting V-sign evolving from English archers proving to the French that they were still able to draw back a bow-string, are now part of the British folk memory.

CAERPHILLY CASTLE

BACKGROUND

In AD 410, as the Romans were abandoning Britain at one end of Europe, at the other end the Emperor Theodosius II began building ingenious new walls to encircle Constantinople, the former Byzantium, now Istanbul in modern Turkey – then the capital of the Eastern Roman Empire.

It took nearly four decades to complete the massive fortifications, but they were not to be breached for nearly eight centuries.

Theodosius's great innovation was the construction of two walls. The walls were about 15 feet (4.5 m) apart, with the inner, at about 30 feet (9 m) tall, much higher than the outer, at about 15 feet (4.5 m). Along the length of both walls were large protruding towers, and a moat was dug in front of the outer wall. There were only five gates in and out of the city.

The new walls proved almost impregnable, the defenders on the higher inner wall being able to fire their arrows safely over the heads of those on the lower, and pick off besiegers from relative safety should the outer wall be overrun. The jutting towers also allowed attackers to be picked off along the outside of the wall itself. Another advantage was that those on the outer wall could sally out to block or pursue attackers, confident those on the inner wall were still holding the defences.

In 1204, during the Fourth Crusade to Palestine, Constantinople fell to the Western Crusaders, who took time out from their 'holy war' against the Muslims in Palestine to attack the city, despite the fact that its occupants were their fellow Christians. Nevertheless they were so impressed by the design that they used it themselves, both back in Europe and in their new conquests in the Holy Land.

Caerphilly Castle was the first concentric, or double walled, castle in Britain, following the design brought back by the Crusaders. It is the largest castle in Wales, the second largest in Britain, after Windsor Castle, and remains one of the largest castles in Europe.

Unlike most of the Welsh castles, which were built by the English King Edward I after his conquest of Wales in 1282, Caerphilly was built by a local Norman warlord, Gilbert 'the Red' de Clare, in 1268–71.

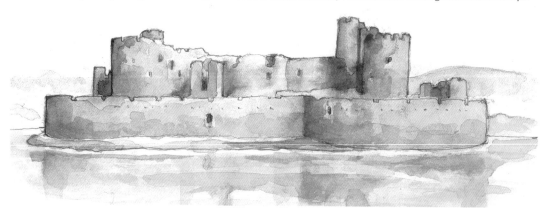

Despite not being built by a King like the other great castles in Wales, Caerphilly remains one of the largest castles in Europe.

In the 5th century, after the departure of the Romans, Wales disintegrated into a patchwork of independent tribal kingdoms. The Norman kings of England allowed powerful warlords to try and 'pacify the Welsh Wildlands' until Edward I finally lost patience in 1282 and formally incorporated the principality into his kingdom.

Gilbert de Clare was just such an opportunistic Norman warlord, in search of land, status and power. He returned from the Crusades in 1268 determined to best Llywelyn (the Last) Prince of Gwynedd from the safety of an ultra-modern concentric castle.

THE WEAPON

Caerphilly Castle is typical of the 13th-century castles being built all over Europe. It is almost perfectly square, has a strong outer wall with bulging, rounded corners, and is moated with a wide artificial lake to impede besiegers and prevent the walls being 'undermined'. Access is limited to two heavily fortified twin-towered gates. Three corners of the higher inner walls are reinforced with protruding cylindrical towers, while the fourth is dominated by the massive keep.

From above, its function is brutally obvious.

WHAT HAPPENED

Llywelyn eventually managed to exasperate King Edward I when he refused five times to deliver the fealty he owed to the Crown. He was stripped of his titles, and his lands were confiscated by the Crown as King Edward invaded and conquered Wales. This vast fortress in South Wales was now redundant. In less accessible North Wales it was a different story. Here Edward was forced to build 10 new castles over the decade spanning 1282–92, during which he employed 8,000 wood cutters, 1,000 navvies, or earth movers, 400 'fine carpenters' and 150 master masons.

In 1403 Caerphilly Castle was taken by the self-styled Prince of Wales, Owen Glendower, exploiting the uncertainties of Henry IV's claim to the throne to establish his own independent principality. Glendower was driven off after one hundred days, only to return two years later with French support. This time he held the castle for over a year.

From then on the castle was of no real strategic importance, though it was damaged by Parliamentary forces in the Civil War of 1642–8.

Having been restored by the Marquess of Bute, it was given to the nation by that family in 1950.

THE THOMAS, THE 'GREAT SHIP' OF EDWARD III

BACKGROUND

In 1349, a fleet of Spanish ships intercepted English merchantmen returning from Bordeaux and stole their cargoes of French wine. This act of flagrant piracy when the two countries were officially at peace enraged the King of England. He prepared his fleet and in particular his 'great ship', the *Thomas*, for battle.

THE WEAPON

King Edward III of England had had to wrestle control of the country from his mother when he was 18. He imprisoned her and executed her lover. It was he who started the Hundred Years War by claiming the throne of France. In 1340 he routed the French fleet at Sluys and then the French army at Crécy in 1346. He also defeated the Scots at Neville's Cross and captured their king. He was commonly regarded as the greatest European warrior of his age, but his country was being ravaged by the Black Death. In just two

On the throne for 50 years, King Edward III was considered such a champion of naval warfare that Parliament accorded him the title 'The King of the Sea'.

years between 1348 and 1350, it was to almost halve the population and there was absolutely nothing he could do to counter the disease. Enemy ships, on the other hand, he could fight, and he was in no mood to be toyed with.

On reports of a fleet of 40 massive Spanish ships, effectively floating castles, entering the Channel, Edward and his son, the Black Prince, led out a fleet of 50 smaller English ships to give battle. Edward was considered the very embodiment of chivalry, which was said to dictate his every thought, word and deed. This encounter with the Spanish was to be no different.

WHAT HAPPENED

At this time war at sea was still very like war on land, and Edward proceeded to deploy the jousting strategy of the mounted knight. He pointed at the largest

THE CODE OF CHIVALRY

Knights in 14th-century Europe attempted to follow the code of Chivalry, sometime called the Decalogue, which consisted of the following ten injunctions:

1. Thou shalt believe all that the Church teaches and shall obey all her commandments.

2. Thou shalt defend the Church.

3. Thou shalt respect all weaknesses and shalt constitute thyself the defender of them.

4. Thou shalt love the country in which thou wast born.

5. Thou shalt not recoil before thine enemy.

6. Thou shalt make war against the Infidel without cessation and without mercy.

7. Thou shalt perform scrupulously thy feudal duties, if they be not contrary to the laws of God.

8. Thou shalt never lie, and shalt remain faithful to thy pledged word.

9. Thou shalt be generous, and give largesse to everyone.

10. Thou shalt be everywhere and always the champion of the Right and the Good against injustice and evil.

LEON GAUTIER, *The Decalogue*

Spanish ship with the words 'I will have tilt with him' and instructed the ship's master to charge straight at it.

The force of the impact felled the Spaniards' mast, and the *Thomas* raced on to engage the next ship.

Though the Spanish, unlike the English, were armed with 'cannon, bars of forged iron and great stones to throw on the enemy and sink him', the battle was principally fought with sword, spear, axe and arrows, and by nightfall it was the English who had won the Battle of Les Espagnols-sur-Mer off the Breton coast and towed 24 captured Spanish ships back to Winchester.

THE CLAYMORE

BACKGROUND

The Gaelic for sword, *Claidheamh*, comes from the Latin word *gladius*, meaning the short, stabbing sword with which Roman legionaries, and gladiators, were armed.

Claidheamh mor means 'great sword' in Gaelic, while *Claidheamh da lamh* means 'two-handed sword'. Scholars still argue about which phrase the word claymore is derived from, or whether it is a mixture of both. The name claymore is applied to two types of Scottish sword: a two-handed sword, used from as early as the 13th century up until the end of the 17th, and the single-handed, basket-hilted weapon which replaced it in the 18th century.

THE WEAPON

The two-handed claymore, used by the Scots against the English and other enemies and in clan warfare from medieval times until the Union with England in 1707, was slightly smaller than other contemporary two-handed swords, with a 13-inch (330 mm) grip, a 42-inch (1.07 m) blade and weighing about 5½ pounds (2.5 kg). The hilt had down-sloping arms often ending in flat 'quatrefoils', like the sign for clubs in a pack of cards. The top of the sword, the end of the grip, was normally set with a large orb. Some claymores were 'clamshell' hilted, the foregrip protected by concave plates and two downward-curving arms making up the crossguard.

From the first Jacobite rebellion in 1715, the word claymore applies to an entirely different type of Scottish sword. Two-handed swords were superseded by single-handed weapons in the 18th century. Accordingly, the Scots adopted a much shorter sword, with a basket hilt to protect the hand and lined with red velvet to soak up blood and sweat, and this was much in evidence in both the Jacobite rebellions of 1715 and 1745.

WHAT HAPPENED

Of the Scottish Highland clansmen rallying behind John Graham of Claverhouse, the first Viscount Dundee, in 1689 in support of the ousted Catholic Stewart king, James II, at the Battle of Killicrankie, many wielded two-handed claymores. This was the last time the two-handed Claymore was used in any number.

Having once served under William of Orange, now the new King, William III, Claverhouse knew his enemy well and achieved a brilliant victory over King William's troops. Unfortunately for the Jacobite cause, his death at the moment of victory deprived the Highlanders of their unifying leader, they reverted to their age-old fratricidal in-fighting, and the opportunities offered by the triumph were squandered.

Adopted by Highland regiments of the British army, the single-handed, basket-hilted claymore was unofficially carried into combat as late as 1945. Captain John Macdonald's famous single-handed capture, in Burma, of a Japanese bunker defended by nine men, armed with rifles, grenades and machine guns, is one such case. Having run out of ammunition, he crawled behind the enemy position, while his wounded comrades distracted the enemy. He killed two and downed one in the doorway with his claymore, before the accidental detonation of their own grenade dealt with the rest.

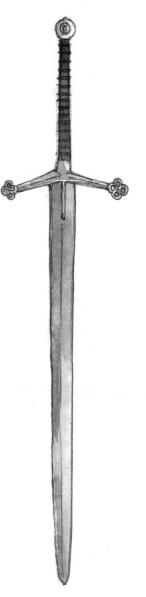

The Scottish two-handed Great Sword, or Claymore, did not survive the Union of the Parliaments between Scotland and England in 1707.

PART II

THE AGE
OF SAIL

PORTHOLES

BACKGROUND

Through his marriage to Elizabeth of York, following his defeat of Richard III at Bosworth in 1485, the new King Henry VII ended 30 years of civil war in England. The Houses of Lancaster and York were finally united – the Wars of the Roses were over. Now Henry could afford to worry less about fighting on English soil and turn his attention to fighting his enemies at sea. He could upgrade his navy. Henry was convinced that the more guns a ship could carry, the more effective it must be in battle. The invention of the naval porthole in roughly 1500 allowed him to put his theory into practice.

With the introduction of the porthole and the true naval broadside British gunners could concentrate on destroying enemy ships rather than the sailors that manned them.

Typically at this time, there were two types of gun: cannons, which were heavy iron tubes, each fastened to a wooden beam, which fired lead or iron shot, or stone cannonballs (though stone shot often cracked in heavy weather); and swivel guns, which were often loaded with gravel and could be swung round on their mountings to shred the enemy personnel.

THE WEAPON

In order to satisfy his master's demand for 'more metal', James Baker, Henry's naval architect, adapted the lower deck cargo doors commonly used by French merchantmen, known as 'gates' or 'portes', to create the portholes through which guns on the lower deck could be deployed, weather permitting.

It was Henry's son, Henry VIII, who exploited this innovation when he built over 85 battleships fitted with over 16 varieties and subvarieties of gun. By doing so, and by championing a new type of long gun, invented by Hans Poppenruyter of Mechelin and tested at Houndsditch, he altered the face of naval gunnery.

WHAT HAPPENED

The guns were designed to cripple ships from a distance, not the sailors or soldiers that manned them, and were to prove invaluable in the contest with the mighty galleons of the Spanish Armada dispatched to subdue his daughter, Elizabeth I.

TUDOR GUNS	BORE (in/mm)	WEIGHT OF GUN (lb/kg)	WEIGHT OF SHOT (lb/kg)
CANNON ROYAL	8½/216	8,000/3,630	66/30
CANNON	8/203	6,000/2,720	60/27
CANNON SERPENTINE	7/178	5,500/2,500	53½/24
BASTARD CANNON	7/178	4,500/2,045	41½/19
DEMI-CANNON	6½/165	4,000/1,820	33½/15
CANNON PETRO	6/152	4,000/1,820	24½/11
CULVERIN	5/127	4,500/2,045	17½/8
BASILISK	5/127	4,500/2,045	15/6.8
DEMI-CULVERIN	4/102	3,400/1,545	9½/4.3
BASTARD CULVERIN	4/102	3,000/1,360	7/3.2
SAKER	3½/89	1,400/635	5½/2.5
MINION	3½/89	1,000/455	4/1.8
FALCON	2½/64	660/300	3/1.36
FALCONET	2/51	500/227	1¼/0.57
SERPENTINE	1½/38	400/182	¾/0.34
RABINET	1/25	300/136	½/0.23

THE GOLDEN HIND

BACKGROUND

In the latter half of the 16th century, the existence of Protestant England and the security of her Queen, Elizabeth I, were under constant threat from Catholic Spain. In the eyes of England's piratical sailors and merchant adventurers, this made the enormous wealth Spain was bringing back from her colonies fair game, whatever conciliatory diplomatic noises may have been emanating from the Queen's court.

In 1577, Francis Drake assembled a squadron of five ships to sail for the River Plate.

THE WEAPON

Drake's ship, the *Golden Hind*, then called the *Pelican*, was the largest ship in the squadron, but even she was only 120 tons and then armed with only five guns of iron and 13 of bronze. The smallest of the five ships was a mere 15 tons.

Despite its small size Drake's *Golden Hind* accomplished one of the greatest maritime triumphs of history.

THE GOLDEN HIND	
DISPLACEMENT	300 tons
LENGTH	120 ft / 37 m
BEAM	18 ft / 5.5 m
DRAUGHT	18 ft / 5.5 m
SPEED	8 knots
CREW	80
ARMAMENT	22 guns (maximum)

WHAT HAPPENED

As the weeks of sailing took their toll, the other four ships either sank or returned home, and the *Pelican*, now renamed the *Golden Hind* after the heraldic beast on the crest of one of Drake's backers, entered the Pacific alone and cruised up the west coast of South America. Sailing unaccompanied in fact worked to Drake's advantage, as the Spanish were simply unable to believe that such a modest vessel on its own could have the audacity to attack the ports and shipping of the current superpower. Certainly none had ever dared to try it before this far from Europe.

Drake's successes were astonishing. In his little ship he managed to plunder Valparaiso, in Chile, and seize a fully-laden galleon. Further up the coast he took two massive consignments of silver, which had been brought from the mines in the Andes and stockpiled at Tarapace, awaiting shipment to Panama. On reaching Lima, in Peru, he seized another galleon with a cargo of gold and precious stones, ballasted with silver.

Spain dispatched an entire fleet to capture Drake and retrieve their treasure. So, instead of returning home the way he came, he had no option but to sail westward across the Pacific and flee back to England by the Cape of Good Hope, sheer necessity forcing him to become the first Englishman to circumnavigate the globe.

Of course, Spain protested to Queen Elizabeth I in the strongest possible terms and, of course, she apologised profusely, expressing outrage at her subject's criminal acts. In reality Drake's stupendous plunder was very welcome in England, the Queen's share paying off all the country's overseas debt with plenty to spare, and despite her vehement recriminations, she knighted him aboard the *Golden Hind* on 4 April 1581. Seven years later Drake would play an important part in seeing off the Spanish Armada.

THE SOVEREIGN OF THE SEAS

BACKGROUND

In 1637 Charles I's master shipwright, Phineas Pett, launched the ship that he had promised the King would be the envy of the world. He turned out to be as good as his word – except with regard to the cost – and the *Sovereign of the Seas* was the prototype for every British capital ship for the next 200 years.

THE SOVEREIGN OF THE SEAS

LAID DOWN	1635
LAUNCHED	1637
DISPLACEMENT	1,522 tons
LENGTH (KEEL)	127 ft / 38.7 m
BEAM	46 ft 6 in / 14.2 m
DEPTH OF HOLD	19 ft 4 in / 5.9 m
ARMAMENT	102 guns at launch
	90 guns in 1642
	100 guns in 1660

Though one of the greatest warships in the history of the world, the *Sovereign of the Seas* would cost Charles I not only his crown but also his head.

THE WEAPON

The *Sovereign of the Seas* had 102 guns on three decks, and an innovative new sail plan involving a topgallant on the mizzenmast and royal sail on the foremast and mainmast. When she was launched, she was the most heavily armed ship in the world and the first true three-decker.

She was not only vast and fast, she was also beautiful, the gilt work and decorative carving alone costing the same as a contemporary warship of 40 guns, a staggering £6,500. It was her gilt work as much as her daunting broadside that led the Dutch to dub her 'The Golden Devil'.

Phineas Pett had promised to build the ship in a year at an estimated cost of £13,680. The keel was laid at Woolwich in December 1635. After 18 months, she was complete but only after an overrun of nearly £28,000. The exact charge was £40,833. 8s. 1½d.

WHAT HAPPENED

In order to meet this massive expense, the King ordered that the already unpopular Ship Money (a tax usually levied on coastal property in time of war) should now be increased and extended inland, which was a way of raising revenue without consulting Parliament.

His actions were questioned in Parliament by the MP John Hampden, contributing to the arguments that eventually led to Civil War and the King's execution.

When Oliver Cromwell was Protector during the Commonwealth, he renamed her the *Sovereign*, and in 1651 she was grounded towards the end of the Battle of Kentish Knock in the First Dutch War. She was rebuilt in 1659. Between 1666 and 1685, now renamed the *Royal Sovereign* by Charles II, she took part in the Four Days Battle, the Battle of St James's Bay, the Battle of Texel and the Battle of Solebay against the Dutch.

In 1685 she was rebuilt again and her horse figurehead was replaced with a lion. She bested the French at the Battles of Beachy Head and Barfleur, but was burnt to the waterline by a careless watchman at Chatham in 1696. Her remaining timbers were re-used to build the new 100-gun *Royal Sovereign*, launched in 1701. She had already changed the course of British naval history.

THE NEW MODEL ARMY, or 'IRONSIDES'

BACKGROUND

The Civil War raged in England between 1642 and 1649. Royalist forces loyal to Charles I, an extravagant, insensitive and whimsical king, who fervently believed in his God-given and exclusive right to rule, fought against their fellow countrymen who supported a Parliament equally convinced of its right to be included in decisions of national importance.

Hastily recruited, expanded and trained, the armies of both sides were disorganised and chaotic. Many regiments were raised, funded and commanded by rich and powerful individuals according to their own personal tastes and practices, and they were often only prepared to serve within striking distance of where they were raised. The commanders,

One of Cromwell's 'Ironsides', or New Model Army troopers, in boots, gauntlet, breastplate and lobster helmet.

unused to taking orders, regularly refused to cooperate with each other, and feuds, contradictory orders and muddle were commonplace.

Oliver Cromwell, a Member of Parliament and cavalryman who commanded the left wing of the Parliamentary army at their victory at the Battle of Marston Moor, was determined to impose professionalism and central control. He pushed the 'Self-denying Ordinance' through Parliament in the autumn of 1644, forcing any member of the House of Commons or the House of Lords to resign his military command. This removed generals who owed their positions of authority in the army to wealth or social standing and allowed them to be replaced with leaders promoted on merit. Cromwell, his son-in-law and two others were effectively exempted from the Self-denying Ordinance by a series of three-month rolling temporary commands, perpetually renewed.

The Parliamentary armies and regiments were then totally reorganised into the 'New Model', Parliament providing standard pay, clothing, equipment and provisions.

THE WEAPON

The 'Souldiers Catechisme' explained what was expected of each soldier and detailed the now universal drill and regulations. The infantry were paid eight pence a day, the cavalry two shillings, though each cavalryman was expected to provide his own horse. All were expected to serve whenever and wherever they were ordered, however personally inconvenient or far from home.

Sir Thomas Fairfax was appointed Captain-General of the New Model Army and requested that Oliver Cromwell be Lieutenant-General of the Horse.

The 22,000 men were divided into 11 regiments of cavalry (6,600 men), 12 regiments of infantry (14,400 men) and one regiment of dragoons (1,000 men). Many of the infantrymen were forcibly 'called up' from the southern and eastern counties, where support for Parliament was strong.

Those officers considered 'unsuitable' because of their religion, behaviour, incompetence or politics were discharged. Cromwell famously declared: 'I would rather have a plain russet-coated Captain that knows what he fights for, and loves what he knows, than that which you call a gentleman and is nothing else.' There was a strong Protestant strain of religious fanaticism in the new army.

The cavalry, Cromwell's troops, were the élite of the New Model Army, just as Prince Rupert of Rhine's cavaliers were the élite of the Royalist.

They wore backplates and breastplates over plain leather 'russet coats', a lobster-tailed helmet with a raisable three-barred visor, a gauntlet on the left hand and thick 'bucket' riding boots.

Despite their light armour, the New Model Cavalry relied on the shock of the charge, normally discharging one of their two loaded pistols just before reaching the enemy and then plunging on in with the sword. Prince Rupert dubbed them 'Ironsides' for the iron-like ability to slice through opposing forces.

One of Prince Rupert's captains described the new cavalry as 'thrice deadly', because they would charge once, then regroup, charge again, then regroup and charge again for yet a third time or chase the enemy from the field, never abandoning the chase to loot or plunder. This was considered astounding, as the wilful Royalist cavaliers, though devastating at the initial charge, were notorious for their lack of discipline and control, afterwards almost invariably careering off in search of booty, rendering them useless for the rest of any battle.

The single regiment of dragoons, used for scouting, patrolling and clearing enemy musketeers, were essentially mounted infantry, armed with flintlocks. In 1650 they were formally converted into proper cavalry.

The New Model Infantry, issued with red coats, consisted of one pikeman, armed with a 16-foot (5-m) pike, to every two musketeers. The pikemen wore pot helmets, backplates and breastplates over their coats, and carried a sword. They led any infantry charge and protected the musketeers from cavalry.

The musketeers wore bandoliers across one shoulder from which hung 12 wooden tubes, each containing a charge of ball and powder for their matchlocks. Arranged in six ranks in combat, the front rank fired then retired to the back to reload, each rank taking the place of the one ahead to maintain fire. Though they sometimes had swords, they did not have bayonets and tended to use the reversed musket as a club at close quarters.

WHAT HAPPENED

The new army took to the battlefield for the first time at Naseby, in Northamptonshire, on 14 June 1645, and routed the King's principal army. In July they were victorious again at Langport, in Somerset. They continued hounding the Royalists out of the West until the King's surrender to the Scots in 1646. The war seemed to be over but, despite all the promises, the army was owed considerable back pay. Waiting for their money, they began to make further demands: indemnity from prosecution for any crimes 'circumstances of war' had forced them to commit; 'one man one vote'; the re-election of Parliament every two years, and the abolition of imprisonment for debt. They marched on London. At the Putney Debates in 1647, they famously insisted that 'the poorest he that is in England hath a life to live as the greatest he'.

In July 1648, Royalist uprisings in Surrey, Kent and Wales forced them to take to the field again, before wiping out an invading Scottish army at Preston. If the King were dead, they argued, such uprisings to reinstate him would not occur. They demanded Charles's execution – and got it.

Between 1649 and 1650 they conquered Ireland, 7,500 of them rewarded with land and remaining as settlers. In Scotland, Charles's son was crowned King Charles II. Led by Cromwell, the outnumbered New Model Army defeated the Scots at Dunbar and Inverkeithing, and then another Royalist army at Worcester in 1651.

With the end of hostilities on English soil, the New Model Army took on the Spanish in Europe and the Caribbean, capturing Jamaica and astonishing contemporary Europeans with the professionalism, efficiency and skills they showed in Flanders.

With the death of Cromwell, however, it was clear that the whole country had had enough of rule by soldier. Nor was there any obvious and capable candidate to step into his shoes. Britain wanted the monarchy back.

General Monck, head of the New Model Army in Scotland, invited Charles II to return as king, which he did in 1660.

The New Model Army, the instrument of the now vilified Parliament, could not be expected to survive the return of its arch-enemy. It was disbanded, except for those of General Monck's regiments that were in attendance to welcome the new king, which survive to this day as the Coldstream Guards and Royal Horse Guards.

THE BROWN BESS

BACKGROUND

Though the Chinese invented gunpowder, which they used for making fireworks and loud bangs, it was an English Franciscan friar from Oxford, Roger Bacon, who first wrote down

the formula in 1250, allowing reliable gunpowder to be produced all over Europe.

The first handguns were matchlocks – in which the gunpowder, rammed into a simple iron tube, was 'touched off' with a lighted 'match', fuse or paper.

These were followed by wheel locks, where the application of a 'match' or flame was replaced with a wheel to make sparks and ignite the powder.

In the later flintlocks, such as the Brown Bess, the 'cock' of the gun struck a flint against iron to make sparks, at the same time exposing the powder in the barrel and firing the charge.

A series of similar flintlock smooth-bore muskets, in use with the British army from the War of the Spanish Succession (1701 – 13) right up until the 1850s, were given the affectionate name 'Brown Bess'. A variety of different sources have been suggested for the name: brown because rusty, like the old Brown Bill, the foot soldiers' long-shafted halberd, that the muskets replaced, with 'Bess' the counterpart to 'Bill'; brown because shiny or burnished, from the Dutch *brun*, meaning shining or bright; or brown because of the colour of the walnut stock, as the stocks of earlier firearms had been painted black. It has even been suggested it got the name from a much-loved camp follower in Canada whose affection for the troops was such that she had to be driven from a garrison at gunpoint.

THE WEAPON

Perhaps the first 'proper' Brown Bess was the Long Land Pattern Flintlock Musket, developed in the 1720s, with a 46-inch (1.17-m) barrel and a wooden ramrod. It was the first British army musket to have brass fittings and gradually evolved over the decades, gaining a double bridle to the lock in 1742 and a steel ramrod, a brass nose-

With an effective range of no more than 150 yards and an effective misfire rate of three out of 10 it was often the bayonet rather than the Brown Bess musket itself that decided the issue when push came to shove.

cap and a new straight lock design in 1746, the year the Scottish Jacobites under Bonnie Prince Charlie were crushed by King George II.

In 1768 the British Army Clothing Warrant attempted to reduce the load of the British infantryman. Uniforms were made less cumbersome and heavy, private soldiers were relieved of their swords, except for Highlanders and Guardsmen, and the musket barrel length was shortened to 42 inches (1.07 m): resulting in the Short Land Musket with a metal ramrod. Production of the Long Land stopped in 1790, and the majority of muskets in use by the British in the Napoleonic Wars were Short Land.

The East India Company had its own private army and created a slightly shorter, lighter weapon with a 39-inch (990-mm) barrel and no thumb plate in 1795. It was taken up by the British Army Board of Ordnance in 1797. Over three million were made, with almost the only modification being a slight reinforcement to the cock in 1809. They were still seeing service with the British army in the 1850s, and one was even caught on film in 1979, being used against invading Soviet tanks in Afghanistan.

Although drill was incessant, unless in action the average musket was unlikely to be actually fired more than a few times a year. The Short Land or India Pattern musket, weighing about 9 pounds (4 kg), could throw a one-ounce lead ball 250 yards (228 m), though effective range when volleying was presumed to be no further than 150 (137). Because of their inaccuracy, firing was normally in formation, at a rate of two or three rounds per minute, although some units managed five. About 30 per cent of shots misfired. At 30 yards (27 m) the ball could penetrate three-eighths of an inch (9.5 mm) of iron or 5 inches (130 mm) of oak. The muskets were equipped with a 14-inch (356 mm) bayonet.

The rolled paper cartridges containing seven drams of powder and a lead ball were sealed with pack thread at each end. To load, the soldier bit off the rear end, poured some powder into the pan as a priming charge and the rest down the barrel, followed by the ball. The paper was then wadded down the barrel with the ramrod to keep it all in place. The gun could then be fired or kept at half-cock. Powder had to be kept dry, and the flints sharp.

WHAT HAPPENED

The expressions 'half-cock', referring to when the soldier failed to fully cock his weapon, 'flash in the pan', when only the primer ignited, failing to set off the main charge, and 'skin flint', when a soldier unable to get new flints had to chip or 'skin' worn ones, all derive from the use of the Brown Bess.

CARRONADES,
or 'THE SMASHERS'

BACKGROUND

The Royal Navy had long been famous for the speed and accuracy with which it could fire its long guns, the shot from a 32-pounder (14.53 kg) gun being capable of penetrating 5 feet (1.5 m) of solid oak at up to 2 miles (3.2 km).

In the 1790s, however, the Carron Company in Scotland developed an entirely new kind of gun called a carronade.

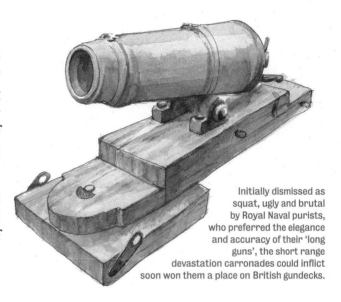

Initially dismissed as squat, ugly and brutal by Royal Naval purists, who preferred the elegance and accuracy of their 'long guns', the short range devastation carronades could inflict soon won them a place on British gundecks.

THE WEAPON

Carronades had the considerable advantage of a minimal recoil, short barrels and a much smaller gun crew, and could, accordingly, be carried by smaller, older or weaker ships than conventional guns of the same gauge. In fact, they enabled such ships to throw a much greater weight of shot than they could possibly have done before.

The downside was their range – a pitiful 100 yards (90 m) – but within that range they were devastating.

The Royal Navy fitted them in several ships for trial purposes, but the debate was still out on their long-term future.

WHAT HAPPENED

When Captain Henry Trollope was given command of the converted merchantman, HMS *Glatton*, he had already summed up his battle tactics on his previous ship, the *Kite*: 'Get close to the enemy and blast!' The *Glatton* carried 56 guns, of which 28 were the new 68-pounder (31 kg) carronades. While cruising off Flanders in July 1795, Trollope single-handedly saw off eight French warships, who allowed him to get up close on the assumption that, as he could not possibly escape, and was hopelessly outnumbered, he must surely be proposing to surrender. On the contrary – he proposed to 'get close to the enemy and blast!'

With broadside after broadside, his enormous shot simply stove in the sides of the enemy ships, sinking one and killing 70 of the crew on another. At nightfall, they turned tail and ran. As a result, the entire British fleet was issued with carronnades, known from then on as 'smashers'.

THE VICTORY

BACKGROUND

The keel of the *Victory*, the fifth ship of the Royal Navy to bear that name, was laid at Chatham in 1759, just a year after the birth of Horatio Nelson, her most famous commander, in a rectory in Norfolk. She took six years to complete and was commissioned in 1778, the same year in which Nelson himself was made a commander.

[handwritten annotations: "1766", "12 YEARS LATER,", "AGE 20?"]

She became Nelson's flagship in 1803. This was the ship on whose quarterdeck he was shot on 21 October 1805 during the Battle of Trafalgar, and in whose cockpit he died four and a half hours after receiving his wound – but not until he had learnt of perhaps the greatest victory the Royal Navy has ever won.

THE WEAPON

The *Victory*'s mainmast reaches 175 feet (53 m) above her deck, the height of Nelson's Column, and the quarterdeck carried twelve 12-pounder (5.45 kg) guns. The forecastle carried two 68-pounder (31 kg) carronades and two more 12-pounders. The upper or main gun deck carried thirty 12-pounder guns, the middle gun deck twenty-eight 24-pounders (10.89 kg), and the lower deck thirty 32-pounders (14.53 kg), each weighing three tons and serviced by 15 men. In all the *Victory* carried 104 guns and had, at Trafalgar, a complement of 850 officers and men.

The Great Guns of the ships at the time of Nelson fired three types of projectile with three

THE VICTORY

LAID DOWN	1759
LAUNCHED	1778
LENGTH	226 ft 6 in / 69 m (bow to stern)
	152 ft 3 in / 47 m (keel)
	186 ft / 57 m (gun deck)
BEAM	51 ft 10 in / 16 m
DEPTH OF HOLD	21 ft 6 in / 6.6 m
TONNAGE	2,162 tons
CREW	850 officers and men
ARMAMENT	104 guns

Though the Royal Navy was not to convert to steam for 50 years, Trafalgar was the last great fleet action of the age of sail.

clearly defined functions: to penetrate the hulls of enemy ships, to shred away sails and rigging, and to mow down enemy personnel.

'Round' or 'solid' shot was the most commonly used for blasting through the sides of opposing ships. A 32-pounder was able to penetrate 5 feet (1.5 m) of solid oak at 2 miles (3.2 km), and at close quarters the guns were double or even treble shotted, compromising accuracy but multiplying the devastation.

Chain-shot was designed to flail through rigging and masts. It was basically two lumps of iron connected by a chain, but there were at least four different types, individual captains and fleets famously championing their own preferrred varieties.

Bar-shot could damage both hulls and rigging and came in a variety of configurations, all incorporating massive weights joined by an iron bar.

Faggot-shot was like a Chinese puzzle of lumps of iron that fitted together to form a perfect cylinder until fired, when they separated in flight to shoot through rope and flesh.

Case-shot, or canister, consisted of a 'can' or 'case' full of iron balls or musket balls that burst out of the cylindrical tin on firing and swept across bows.

Grape-shot was a canvas bag of two-pound cast-iron balls, separated into three levels by iron plates, which had the effect of an enormous blunderbuss or punt gun.

Elongating shot looked like two iron hammers connected by rings at either end, which elongated and twisted and turned in flight to crash through wood, rope, canvas and people.

Ships in the Royal Navy were classified by the number of guns they carried and 'rated'. The *Victory* was a first-rater, a three-decker with 100 guns or more. Only first-, second- or third-rated ships, those over 74 guns, were deemed fit for the line of battle, otherwise known as battleships.

RATES IN NELSON'S NAVY			
RATE	No. OF GUNS	WEIGHT OF BROADSIDE	No. OF MEN
FIRST	100 or more	2,550–2,500 lb / 1,158–1,135 kg	850–950
SECOND	98 or 90	2,300–2,050 lb / 1,044–931 kg	750
THIRD	80 or 74	1,970–1,764 lb / 894–801 kg	720 or 640
FOURTH	64 or 50	1,200–800 lb / 545–363 kg	490 or 350
FIFTH	44, 40, 38, 36 or 32	636–350 lb / 289–159 kg	320–250
SIXTH	28, 24 or 20	280–250 lb / 127–113 kg	200–260

WHAT HAPPENED

Perhaps Nelson's three most famous victories are the Battle of the Nile, Copenhagen and, of course, Trafalgar.

Before the Battle of the Nile in 1798, aboard his ship HMS *Vanguard*, Nelson said, 'By this time tomorrow I shall have gained a peerage or Westminster Abbey.' His 14 ships took on the French in the Bay of Aboukir on the Egyptian coast. Though wounded in the head by shrapnel, he destroyed or captured 11 enemy ships, leaving Napoleon's army stranded in Egypt.

'Victory,' said Nelson afterwards, 'is not a name strong enough for such a scene.'

In 1801, at the Battle of Copenhagen, he took on the Danes aboard his HMS *Elephant*. When his commander-in-chief, Admiral Sir Hyde Parker, ordered him to retreat, he ignored the signal with the words, 'I have only one eye – I have a right to be blind sometimes – I really do not see the signal.' After he had broken the Danish defensive line, they agreed to an armistice.

But it was for Trafalgar that Nelson gained the greatest accolade. On the eve of the battle, in which he was to meet the combined French and Spanish fleets just outside the Strait of Gibraltar, he prayed:

> MAY THE GREAT GOD, WHOM I WORSHIP, GRANT TO MY COUNTRY AND FOR THE BENEFIT OF EUROPE IN GENERAL, A GREAT AND GLORIOUS VICTORY; AND MAY NO MISCONDUCT IN ANYONE TARNISH IT; AND MAY HUMANITY IN VICTORY BE THE PREDOMINANT FEATURE OF THE BRITISH FLEET.
>
> FOR MYSELF, INDIVIDUALLY, I COMMIT MY LIFE TO HIM WHO MADE ME, AND MAY HIS BLESSING LIGHT UPON MY ENDEAVOURS FOR SERVING MY COUNTRY FAITHFULLY. TO HIM I RESIGN MYSELF AND THE JUST CAUSE WHICH IS ENTRUSTED TO ME TO DEFEND. AMEN.

Having sent the signal, 'England expects that every man will do his duty' (his original message was 'England confides', but the signalman had difficulty with the word confides, so it was changed to expects), he split the enemy force in two, sank one ship and captured 17.

At the height of battle, noting that in his extravagant uniform and decorations he was the target for every enemy sharpshooter within range, his officers urged him to cover his medals. 'In honour I gained them,' he said, 'and in honour I will die with them.' He did.

This was the last great fleet action of the age of sail, saving Britain from invasion for the rest of the Napoleonic Wars and confirming her mastery of the Seven Seas for at least a century. It was this mastery of the seas, and thus her ability to trade, that allowed Britain to finance her eventual defeat of Napoleon.

The Victory became the flagship of Portsmouth Command in 1825 and was restored to her Trafalgar condition in 1928. She still lies in No. 2 Dock, Portsmouth.

These were the eight orders that preceded the firing of a Great Gun:

'SILENCE!
CAST LOOSE YOUR GUNS!
LEVEL YOUR GUNS!
OUT TOMPIONS!
PRIME!
RUN OUT YOUR GUNS!
POINT YOUR GUNS!
FIRE!'

THE BAKER RIFLE

BACKGROUND

The Baker rifle was the first purpose-built British rifle commissioned by the British army. It was designed to be easy to load, fire and maintain, as well as strong, reliable and 'mass-production friendly'.

Hunting rifles had been in existence for nearly a century, and the British Colonel Patrick Ferguson had designed a breech-loading rifle in 1774, but it was not until 1800 that the Board of Ordnance made the decision to issue rifles to the British army.

Previously, British soldiers had been trained in delivering concentrated musket volleys at short range as quickly as possible. Accuracy was not considered a priority, as massed infantry fired on massed infantry, and the sheer weight of lead ploughing into the advancing enemy would cause indiscriminate general carnage until the severely mauled opposing troops either fled or the issue was decided at the point of a bayonet.

Drill, discipline and the stomach to remain steady under fire were what decided battles, it was believed – not individual sharpshooters picking off carefully selected targets. It was the American War of Independence that gave the British grounds for a rethink.

The 'rifling' of a rifle, the twisted ridges and grooves on the inside of its barrel, gives spin to the departing bullet, making it more stable in flight and far more accurate than a smooth-bore musket ball.

The American farmers, trappers and hunters, armed with the same rifles they used daily to kill game, proved deadly against the musket-bearing British infantry in the late 1770s. In the 1790s, French Revolutionary skirmishers, also armed with rifles, reinforced the lessons the British learnt in America. As a result, in 1797, Parliament bought 5,000 hunting rifles from Prussia. They were not a success. Not only were they of differing bore sizes, causing confusion over the issuing of ammunition, but also, because single shots were the norm with hunting rifles, they were slow to load and needed frequent cleaning. It was decided that a purpose-built British rifle must be produced.

On 4 February 1800, leading British gunmakers submitted their rifle designs for the Board of Ordnance trials at Woolwich.

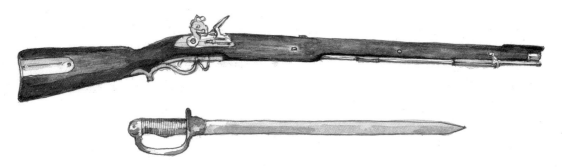

When introduced, the Baker Rifle was at least three inches shorter than a standard musket and accordingly it was fitted with a two-foot sword bayonet to maintain the reach of riflemen at close quarters.

THE WEAPON

The contract was won by Ezekiel Baker, who already supplied pistols and muskets to the army and the East India Company, and was known to the Prince of Wales.

After some initial modifications, moving away from the musket pattern and towards that of a German Jäger rifle, it was decided that the rifle should be .625-inch (15.8 mm) calibre, with a 30-inch (760-mm) barrel, weighing 9 pounds (4.08 kg), the same weight as a 'Brown Bess' musket. It had a folding backsight, walnut stock and brass 'butt trap'. The comparative shortness of the rifle – it was only 45 inches (1.14 m) long, compared to most muskets which were nearly 5 feet (1.5 m) – meant that a longer, 24-inch (609-mm) bayonet was required if the rifleman was to hold his own in close combat.

WHAT HAPPENED

The army had insisted that the Baker had to be accurate up to at least 200 yards (183 m), but the Baker could do much better than this. Rifleman Thomas Plunkett of the 1st Battalion 95th Rifles shot the French General Colbert at 800 yards (732 m) during the British retreat to Corunna in the Peninsular War, and then the General's aide, who was looking down aghast at his stricken superior.

Between the Battle of Trafalgar in 1805 and the Battle of Waterloo in 1815, about 20,000 Baker rifles were produced in Birmingham and London, undergoing various modifications.

From 1840, having proved the value of rifles to the British High Command, the Baker rifle was gradually replaced with the Brunswick rifle.

THE MARTELLO TOWER

BACKGROUND

Martello towers are round, defensive sea forts, rarely over 40 feet (12 m) high, built all over the British Empire between 1804 and 1850, as far afield as Australia, Canada, the West Indies, Mauritius and Sierra Leone. Of the 140 that were built in all, only one was ever captured, and that by fellow Britons, at Cork Harbour in Ireland, during the Fenian uprising of 1867.

This impregnable bastion of the British Empire was inspired by an enemy equivalent.

As early as the 15th century, circular defensive sea towers had been constructed around the coast of Corsica, first by local people and then the Genovese, when they ruled the island, as a defence against North African pirates. They were normally two storeys high, about 40 feet (12 m) across, with no windows and a single doorway set into the wall, 16 feet (5 m) above the ground. The entrance ladder could be drawn inside in the event of attack. The approach of suspicious shipping was signalled by a beacon on the roof. The Genovese improved and updated this local innovation.

In the winter of 1794, when Britain was at war with France, two of her finest warships were dispatched to take the tower off Mortella Point in Corsica. It must have seemed an almost trivial straightforward mission, but to the astonishment of the Royal Navy, the

The high-tech navies of the late 18th century were staggered that the primitive structure that had evolved four centuries earlier could still hold its own against the most up- to-date modern warships.

British public and perhaps even the Corsicans themselves, HMS *Fortitude*, of 74 guns, and HMS *Juno*, of 32 guns, totally failed in their objective. Despite being bombarded for two and a half hours by both ships, the 33 defenders in the tower kept up a continuous and deadly accurate fire of shot heated red hot by the tower's furnace. The *Fortitude* was very nearly sunk, and the tower was only captured by Sir John Moore's soldiers after two days of desperate fighting, and then only when a lucky strike from the British soldiers' own hot shot set the tower on fire. Only two of the defenders were even wounded. Vice-Admiral Hood's flabbergasted report reads as follows:

> THE FORTITUDE AND JUNO WERE ORDERED AGAINST IT, WITHOUT MAKING THE LEAST IMPRESSION BY A CONTINUED CANNONADE OF TWO HOURS AND A HALF: AND THE FORMER SHIP BEING VERY MUCH DAMAGED BY RED HOT SHOT, BOTH HAULED OFF. THE WALLS OF THE TOWER WERE OF A PRODIGIOUS THICKNESS ... AND ALTHOUGH IT WAS CANNONADED FROM THE HEIGHT FOR TWO DAYS, WITHIN 150 YARDS, AND APPEARED IN A VERY SHATTERED STATE, THE ENEMY STILL HELD OUT.

The Admiralty was staggered and hugely impressed. Nevertheless, when they ordered the building of copies they spelt the name of Mortella wrong, muddling the order of the vowels – and the misspelling stuck.

THE WEAPON

Of similar dimensions to the one at Mortella, the British Martello towers were built with three storeys and sometimes a cellar. Storerooms and magazines were on the ground floor, while half of the first floor was occupied by the 24 men and the other half by their officer. The roof boasted one or two heavy cannon that could rotate as required.

WHAT HAPPENED

General William Twiss supervised the building of over 100 Martello towers along the south and east coasts of England, Ireland, Jersey and Guernsey between 1804 and 1812, as a defence against invasion from Napoleonic France. Another 40 were built overseas. The last tower to be built, Fort Denison in Sydney, Australia, was completed in 1857, after which the increasing power and rifling of naval guns meant they were no longer impregnable. Many rendered valuable service in the Second World War as observation posts and mounts for anti-aircraft guns.

THE KUKRI

BACKGROUND

The Seven Years War, which ended in 1763, saw France ejected from India. As the British Honourable East India Company took advantage of this opportunity for expansion, it came into increasing conflict with the city state of Gorkha, in western Nepal, which eventually controlled a kingdom stretching from Kashmir to Bhutan. In 1814 the governor-general declared war on Nepal, launching two campaigns which finally ended with a peace treaty in 1816.

During the two years of battle the British and Gurkha soldiers had learnt to respect and admire each other and, once peace was established, Gurkha volunteers were recruited into the Honourable East India Company's army.

Uniquely, these troops were armed with a short, curved hacking dagger, called a kukri.

THE WEAPON

The kukri has been described as 'the marriage of the knife to the axe'. The Siropate kukris, with a thinner blade, are designed for war, Budhuni kukris for chopping wood. The war kukri is a short, hacking sword which can also be used as a tool. The kukri blade is normally 2–4 inches (50–100 mm) wide and 7–10 inches (175–250 mm) long. They have a heavy spine and a single, hard-tempered cutting edge. Chopping efficiency is enhanced by the 20-degree 'crook' in the blade, giving the distinctive boomerang shape, though kukris are not designed to be thrown.

It became a tradition that kukris should be forged from the steel leaf springs of a British army lorry. The spike continuing from the back of the blade passes right through the handle, which is made of hard wood or water buffalo horn. When finished, a kukri should balance perfectly on a rifle barrel.

The wooden fighting sheath is covered with black leather and also accommodates two small tools – a small cutting knife, called a karda, and a blunt chakmak for sharpening the kukri and striking sparks for fire. Old scabbards often had a pocket for tinder or flints.

Kukris also have religious significance. Hindu ceremonies to bless the kukris are held during the Dasain sacrificial festival.

Kukris have a pair of notches just before the blade meets the handle, called the kanra or cho, which represent the Goddess Kali. They also guide blood off the blade before it reaches the handle. Kukri blades also have two gouges running just below the spine, called the chirra, representing the spear of the God Shiva, and the the aunlo bal, the 'finger of strength'.

The knifesmiths, or kamis, are members of the 'untouchable' caste and are also called biswakarma, 'worldmakers'. Gurkha soldiers are members of the Kshatriya caste.

Like the Saxon seax, the Turkish *yataghon* and the Greek *kopis*, when not used for fighting the kukri is a versatile tool, doubling as axe and machete. It has also come to symbolize some of the greatest fighting men , the Gurkhas, the world has ever known.

WHAT HAPPENED

From the Pindaree War in 1817, the Sikh Wars and the Indian Mutiny right through to the present day, the reputation of the Gurkha regiments for ferocity, courage, gallantry and honour has gone from strength to strength. The mere knowledge that they are present causes the hearts of their enemies to sink.

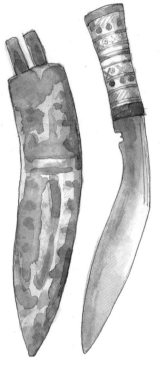

The Gurkha Kukri has been described as the marriage of the axe to the knife; both a weapon and a tool.

THE ROYAL NAVAL FRIGATE

BACKGROUND

The Royal Navy frigate evolved from the small galley known as a 'frigata', used for scouting and carrying messages in Tudor times. Over time, the frigata took on a second deck over the oars and began to carry guns.

The first ship to be formally designated a frigate was the *Constant Warwick*, built by Peter Pett in 1646. Pett's design provided a much more stable gun deck but still included a bank of oars on either side.

By the 1750s, the frigate without oars had evolved, with between 20 and 44 guns. Fast, elegant, nimble ships of the fifth or sixth rate, the new frigates were invaluable for probing, scouting and provoking the enemy, for running errands and delivering orders. By the Napoleonic Wars at least 200 were in service with the Royal Navy.

The dashing, courageous captains of these beautiful ships, often at the beginning of illustrious careers, captured the imagination of the British public, not least, after the French Revolution, through the vast amounts of prize money they were often able to accumulate through the capture of enemy merchantmen or the recapturing of British cargo ships taken by the French.

Since the American War of Independence of 1776–83, Britain's relationship with America had been at best ambivalent. After the victory at Trafalgar confirmed Britain's mastery of the seas in 1805, the Royal Navy behaved towards America with increasing contempt, stopping and searching her ships and regularly impressing her seamen (abducting them from American ships and forcing them to join the Royal Navy). In June 1812, unable to bear these insults any longer, America allied herself with France and declared war on Britain.

Though British forces on land achieved some success, which included burning down the White House, at sea it was a different story. To the astonishment and shame of the Royal Navy, when frigate met frigate, the better-paid volunteer American sailors seemed more than a match for their older cousins. The newer and much bigger American frigates were apparently better handled than their British equivalents, which they initially outsailed and

Though smaller, older, under-manned and far from home, British Frigates on the American station, like HMS *Shannon*, were more than a match for the Americans in dash and courage.

outgunned while inflicting a series of humiliating defeats. The fact that the cream of the Royal Navy frigates were in European waters was neither here nor there to a British public used to inevitable victory. The USS *Constitution* took HMS *Guerriere* and HMS *Java*. The USS United States beat HMS *Macedonian*. It was left to Philip Broke, captain of the 38-gun HMS *Shannon*, to put things right.

THE WEAPON

HMS SHANNON

LAID DOWN	1805	**ARMAMENT**	
LAUNCHED	1806	**UPPER DECK**	28 x 18-pdr (8.17 kg) guns
IN SERVICE	1806–59	**QUARTERDECK**	1 x long 6-pdr (2.72 kg) gun
DISPLACEMENT	951 tons		2 x 9-pdr (4.08 kg) guns
LENGTH	150 ft 2 in / 45.8 m		2 x 12-pdr (5.45 kg) carronades
BEAM	39 ft 11 in / 12.2 m		1 x 12-pdr (5.45 kg) boat carronade
CREW	330		14 x 32-pdr (14.53 kg) carronades
		FORECASTLE	2 x 9-pdr (4.08 kg) guns
			2 x 32-pdr (14.53 kg) carronades

WHAT HAPPENED

In 1813, on finding the recently refitted USS *Chesapeake* lying in Massachusetts Bay, Captain Broke sent in the following challenge:

> AS THE CHESAPEAKE APPEARS NOW READY FOR SEA, I REQUEST YOU WILL DO ME THE FAVOUR TO MEET THE SHANNON WITH HER, SHIP TO SHIP, TO TRY THE FORTUNE OF OUR RESPECTIVE FLAGS …
>
> I ENTREAT YOU, SIR, DO NOT IMAGINE THAT I AM URGED BY MERE PERSONAL VANITY TO THE WISH OF MEETING THE CHESAPEAKE: OR THAT I DEPEND ONLY ON YOUR PERSONAL AMBITION FOR YOUR ACCEDING TO THIS INVITATION. WE BOTH HAVE NOBLER MOTIVES. FAVOUR ME WITH A SPEEDY REPLY. WE ARE SHORT OF PROVISIONS AND WATER AND CANNOT STAY LONG.

The gallant American captain of the 43-gun *Chesapeake* landed five of his guns to even the match (the *Shannon* having 38, excluding carronades) and, trailing a tail of American support craft and reporters anxious not to miss the next humiliation of the antiquated and despotic British, sailed to within 100 yards (91 m) of the *Shannon*.

Eleven minutes after the first broadside was fired at 35 yards (32 m), the duel was over. Captain Lawrence of the *Chesapeake*, fatally wounded, had been carried below with the words, 'Sink her. Do not give up the ship.' Nevertheless, the British boarding party, led by Captain Broke, overwhelmed the American crew and the *Chesapeake* was taken in tow by the *Shannon*, who sailed her triumphantly to the safety of a British port in Canada.

The natural order – and the Royal Navy's reputation – had been restored.

THE RATTLER AND THE BLACK PRINCE

BACKGROUND

By the 1850s, the Royal Navy was the only sea power of any consequence not to be considering iron plating for the decks and hulls of Britain's warships. Perhaps this was not surprising, as the Royal Navy had been equally slow to accept the superiority of steam power over sail, arguing that vast paddle wheels on either side of steam merchantmen necessarily reduced the number of guns in a warship's broadside. The paddle wheels themselves were also exceptionally vulnerable in battle.

As far as the use of iron was concerned, the reservations centred on the difficulty of repairing it in the heat of action. Holes made by roundshot in solid oak were also easily plugged by sheet lead, while iron was ripped into twisted rents which were difficult to seal with any speed.

Despite the introduction of steam engines and screw propellers it took decades for the British Admiralty to entirely abandon the beauty and familiarity of masts and rigging.

The screw propeller seemed to do away with the objections to the steam engine, by removing the necessity for paddle wheels, but still the Admiralty prevaricated, and eventually a tug-of-war was proposed to settle the matter once and for all. On 3 April 1845, HMS *Rattler*, the first warship in the world with a screw propeller, took on the paddle steamer HMS *Alecto*.

Despite all the *Alecto*'s giant paddle wheels could do, the *Rattler*'s underwater screw propeller dragged her backwards at 2½ knots. The debate was over.

It was another 10 years, however, before the Royal Navy was convinced of the benefits of iron in warship construction, and this time it took a humiliating lesson from their old enemy the French. In the Crimean War of 1854–6, precipitated by the Russian occupation of parts of the Ottoman Empire, which the French and British saw as the start of Russian expansion into Europe, the Russian land batteries were equipped with explosive shells. While the oak hulls of British warships were reduced to sodden splinters, some of the French ships were armoured with 4-centimetre plates of iron and escaped virtually unscathed.

THE WEAPON

In 1860, after the French had launched their first fully-armoured ship, the *Gloire*, described as 'an iron lion amid a flock of wooden sheep', Britain launched the world's first all-metal-hulled ships, the *Black Prince* and the *Warrior* – the 'ironclads'.

WHAT HAPPENED

From 1860 all new Royal Navy warships were built with iron cladding and screw propellers. The Admiralty also switched from muzzle- to breech-loaded rifled guns, increasing the accurate range by 10 miles (16 km) and the weight of projectile by over 20 times.

THE BLACK PRINCE

LAID DOWN	1860
LAUNCHED	1861
SPEED	13.6 knots
BEAM	58 ft / 18 m
DISPLACEMENT	9,210 tons
DRAUGHT	27 ft / 8.2 m
LENGTH	380 ft / 116 m

THE 1853 ENFIELD RIFLED MUSKET

BACKGROUND

One and a half million .577-calibre, muzzle-loaded Enfield rifled muskets were produced at the Royal Small Arms Factory at Enfield between 1853 and 1867, when they were replaced for British imperial forces by the cartridge-loaded Snider-Enfield rifle.

THE WEAPON

The 1853 Enfield rifles were officially designated 'rifled muskets' to reassure the British infantrymen of the time that the new rifles were the same length as the muskets they replaced. This 'reach' was considered essential, both for bayonet fighting and so that the muzzles of the second rank of soldiers 'reached' past the faces of the men in front. The barrel was bound on to the forepiece with three metal loops or 'bands', so that the rifle is often now called the three-band musket.

The muzzle-loaded rifle, in capable hands, could fire at least three aimed shots a minute with an effective range of 300 yards (270 m). With a 39-inch (990-mm) barrel and a total length of 53 inches (1.35 m), the rifle weighed nine pounds and five ounces.

WHAT HAPPENED

The Enfield rifle was used throughout the British Empire from 1853 onwards, seeing extensive action in the Crimean War (1854–6) and the New Zealand Land Wars between 1845 and 1872.

It was also the second most widely used infantry weapon in the American Civil War after the Springfield Model 1861 Rifled Musket.

Issuing the 1853 Enfield Rifled Musket to Indian sepoys in 1856 was eventually to trigger the Indian Mutiny of 1857.

It was imported by both sides until, seeing that the Confederates were doomed to defeat, the British government banned sales to the South.

In 1856 the Honourable East India Company, which effectively ruled British India, issued the 1853 Enfield rifled musket to its sepoys, the Indian soldiers.

In order to load the weapon, the sepoys were required to bite the end off the paper cartridge, pour the 68 grains of black powder down the barrel and ram it home with the empty paper cartridge case, followed by the ball.

Some regiments of sepoys became convinced that the paper cartridge was greased with pig fat (unclean to Muslims) and cow fat (sacred to Hindus). Although this was not true, the British officers' suggestion that they make up their own cartridges using inoffensive beeswax was taken as proof that the cartridges really were contaminated.

Perhaps encouraged by the prophecy that British rule in India would end one hundred years after Robert Clive's famous victory at Plassey in 1757, in 1857 the sepoys in Meerut in northern India refused to load their cartridges, killed their officers and triggered a mass rebellion against British rule.

After hideous atrocities on both sides, the mutiny was suppressed and the British Government took over the administration of India from the East India Company in 1858.

PART III

MACHINE GUNS
to MILLS BOMBS

THE MAXIM GUN

BACKGROUND

Introduced in 1886 by British engineer Hiram Maxim (1840–1916), the Maxim gun was the first self-powered machine gun. Instead of the multiple barrels and hand cranks used by the earlier Gatling and Gardner guns, the Maxim used the energy from the firing of each bullet to eject the empty cartridge and insert a new one.

THE WEAPON

Firing 600 rounds per minute, which was 30 times faster than a bolt-action rifle and almost seven times faster than a Gatling gun, the Maxim gun has been credited with speeding up the colonisation of Africa, by enabling Western forces to annihilate less well armed opponents in pitched battle. The British Vickers, German Maschinengewehr and Russian Pulemyot machine guns that were to cause such carnage in the First World War were essentially modified Maxims.

The Maxim could be operated by one man, although teams of two were normal and, with its belt feed and tripod, it did away with the horsedrawn gun carriages and hoppers of ammunition necessary for the earlier hand-cranked guns.

Hiram Maxim demonstrated his first prototype in October 1884. His Maxim Gun Company, which was financed by Albert Vickers, had a factory at Hatton Garden in London and eventually merged with Vickers.

WHAT HAPPENED

The Maxim was first used in combat during the Emin Pasha Relief Expedition led by Henry Morton Stanley in the late 1880s.

In October 1888, the new commander-in-chief of the British army, Sir Garnet Wolseley, ordered 120 Maxims, which could take the same ammunition as the standard British army rifle. During the First Matabele War of 1893–4, fifty British soldiers armed with four Maxims fought off 5,000 Matabeles. It was to prove equally devastating at Omdurman in 1898. In the Boer War, a large calibre version, firing a 1-pound (0.45 kg) shell, known as the pom-pom, was used by both sides.

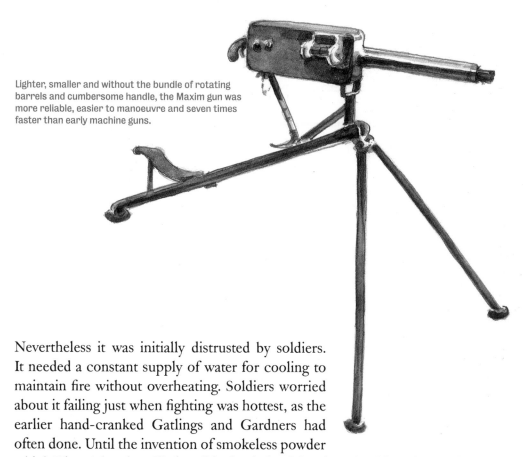

Lighter, smaller and without the bundle of rotating barrels and cumbersome handle, the Maxim gun was more reliable, easier to manoeuvre and seven times faster than early machine guns.

Nevertheless it was initially distrusted by soldiers. It needed a constant supply of water for cooling to maintain fire without overheating. Soldiers worried about it failing just when fighting was hottest, as the earlier hand-cranked Gatlings and Gardners had often done. Until the invention of smokeless powder which Hiram's brother, Hudson Maxim, helped develop, the thick clouds of black powder smoke generated by the firing of 600 rounds a minute also instantly gave away the location of the gun in battle.

It was not long, however, before the Maxim, or one of the many copies, was the staple of most modern armies. Almost half of all casualties in the Russo-Japanese War of 1905 were inflicted by Maxim guns. It was seen as so instrumental in the Communist takeover of Russia that Lenin himself was depicted manning a Maxim in Soviet propaganda.

For several years in the First World War, the descendants of this feverish weapon of defence dominated the battlefields, until the British invention of the tank swung the pendulum back in favour of attack.

THE WEBLEY REVOLVER

BACKGROUND

The Webley Pistol Mk I was adopted by the British army on 8 November 1887, 20,000 revolvers being ordered at a cost of £3. 1s. 1d. each.

The Birmingham-based firm of Webley & Scott specifically designed the .455-inch (11.5- mm) calibre 'Self Extracting Revolver' to replace the Enfield Mark I and II revolvers, then in use with the British army, which did not have a practical extraction mechanism for spent cartridges.

THE WEAPON

Weighing 2¼ pounds (1.02 kg) and nearly 12 inches (305 mm) long, with a six-round cylinder and an effective range of 50 yards (45 m), the new 'top break' Webley revolver was designed so that opening or 'breaking' the pistol automatically removed the spent cartridges from the cylinder. With the .455 Webley cartridge, it remains one of the most powerful 'top break' revolvers ever produced. The First World War Mark VI was regarded as virtually indestructible, and some were adapted to take a modified French Pritchard bayonet. The Prideaux speedloading device dramatically increased sustained rates of fire under pressure.

WHAT HAPPENED

The 1899 Mark IV was bought by many British commissioned and non-commissioned officers on their way out to the Second Boer War and, as a consequence, is often now called the Boer War Model.

The Webley Marks IV, V and VI were the standard sidearms for British and Commonwealth troops in the First World War. They were issued to officers and airmen, tank and machine gun crews, boarding parties and trench raiders.

Between the two World Wars, the British Army concluded that a smaller calibre bullet would be just as effective as the .455, and would also allow a smaller weapon.

Accordingly, Webley developed the .38/200 calibre Mark IV revolver, almost identical to the .455 Mark VI, but on a smaller scale to match the smaller cartridge.

The Royal Small Arms Factory at Enfield produced an almost identical weapon themselves very soon after, but in which none of the parts could be used in the Webley. In response Webley sued the British government for £2,250, the cost of research and design – and though they did not win the case, they were awarded half their

Throughout the British Empire the classic Webley revolver was a symbol of military leadership in the field for at least half a century.

costs, £1,250, in 'recognition of their design work'. The Enfield Revolver No.2 Mark I was adopted by the British Government, and the Mark I* and Mark I**, but production problems meant the Webley was issued as the standard sidearm, in much greater numbers, and remained in service around the world until the 1970s.

THE LEE ENFIELD RIFLE

BACKGROUND

The Lee Enfield was the British army's standard bolt-action, magazine-fed, repeating rifle for over half a century. Introduced in November 1895, it superseded the earlier Martini-Henry, Martini-Enfield and Lee-Metford rifles and saw continuous service until the 1950s. The 'Lee' in Lee Enfield refers to James Paris Lee's rear-locking bolt system and the 'Enfield' to the Royal Small Arms Factory at Enfield.

THE WEAPON

The Lee Enfield took a box magazine for ten .303-inch (7.7-mm) cartridges, loaded manually from above, either by five-round chargers or one round at a time. The Lee bolt-action and the detachable sheet-steel, 10-round, double-column magazine made it the fastest military bolt-action rifle of its time.

The first Lee Enfield, with its characteristic walnut stock, was introduced in November 1895. This was the .303-calibre rifle, 'Magazine, Lee Enfield' or MLE, known as 'Emily'. It was quickly followed in 1896 by a shorter version with a 21-inch (533-mm) rather than 30-inch (760-mm) barrel.

In 1904 the 'Short, Magazine, Lee Enfield', the SMLE or 'Smelly', was introduced with a 25-inch (635-mm) barrel, which in turn led on to the classic SMLE Mark III in January 1907 with a simplified rear sight, improved hand-guards, and magazines and chamber adapted for the new Mark VII High Velocity Spitzer .303 shell. Weighing 8.8 pounds (4 kg), the Smelly Mark III had an overall length of 44.5 inches (1.13 m). To facilitate wartime mass-production, the Mark III was slightly modified into the Mark III*.

The next major evolution was lighter, stronger and easier to mass-produce. The 'Rifle, No. 4 Mark I' had a barrel continuing on from the forepiece, and a spike bayonet, known as a 'pig-sticker', until popular demand forced the production of an alternative bladed bayonet. The 'Rifle, No. 4 Mk II', which appeared after the war, had a beech stock and brass butt plates. Working examples of all these models are still in use today.

WHAT HAPPENED

Sergeant Snoxall of the British army set the world record when he hit a 12-inch (305-mm) target at 300 yards (270 m) with 38 rounds in 59½ seconds in 1914. Effective range was considered to be 550 yards (503 m), though astonishing lethal accuracy was achieved at distances of almost 2,000 yards (1,830 m).

In the First World War the concentrated British rifle fire of the SMLE Mark III rifles was repeatedly mistaken by Germans for that of machine guns.

Over 17 million Lee Enfields were made in various permutations and, although phased out in the UK in the late 1950s, replaced by the L1A1 self-loading rifle, it remains standard issue for many armies and police forces in the Commonwealth, the longest-serving bolt-action rifle still in official use today.

For 75 years basic military training in the British Commonwealth began with an introduction to the Lee Enfield Rifle.

HMS DREADNOUGHT

BACKGROUND

In the early 20th century, the most powerful nations on the globe were jockeying for supremacy at sea. For 100 years, since her victory at Trafalgar, Britain had quite literally ruled the waves, stamping out the slave trade and policing the sea lanes that connected the largest empire the world had ever seen.

To Britain at least, this seemed entirely natural, if not inevitable, but as other nations caught up industrially, so they began to build and re-equip their own navies with much larger, faster and better armed ships. The building programmes of France and Germany were a particular worry to the British Admiralty. Britain had 40 capital ships in 1905, a third of all the capital ships in the world, but it seemed that it would not be long before the other nations caught her up.

Philip Watts, the naval designer and general manager of Armstrong & Co. at Elswick-on-Tyne, the foremost warship yard in the world, had long dreamt of an entirely new class of battleship, going right back to first principles and incorporating all the latest scientific advances: a class of battleship that would make all previous warships obsolete.

Between 1884 and 1902 he built ships for the navies of Japan, Argentina, Brazil, Chile, Norway, Italy, Portugal, Romania, Turkey and, of course, Britain – refining and honing his dream.

In 1902 Watts was appointed the Director of Naval Construction at the Admiralty, and in 1904 Admiral John Fisher, who had been discussing the theoretical new battleships with Watts for 25 years, became First Sea Lord. Together they determined to create what they had so often talked about – their 'ship of dreams'– which was eventually to be launched in 1906.

THE WEAPON

One of the key ingredients of the new invincible battleship was the marine turbine. Convinced that marine turbines were a massive improvement on the coal-fed reciprocating engines then in use, a private individual, Charles Parsons, spent a fortune trying to convince the Admiralty that this was so. He was resolutely ignored. At the Royal Naval Review of

1897, he forced their hand. His little craft *Turbinia* had the audacity to potter out to the vast anchored warships, under the very noses of the horrified reviewing admirals, and weave its way between them. A fast destroyer was dispatched to intercept the irksome interloper, but as the two boats were about to meet, the *Turbinia* suddenly engaged her marine turbines and bounded away at the then unheard-of speed of 30 knots. The 'ship of dreams' would have marine turbines.

Laid down in 1905, HMS *Dreadnought* was built in 366 days in total secrecy and proved to cost less than her predecessors, both to build and then to run. No existing battleship had more than four 12-inch (305-mm) guns at this time. HMS *Dreadnought* had ten 12-inch guns in five turrets, three down the central line and one on each flank. She could bring six guns to bear straight ahead or astern, or deliver a broadside from eight. She had another 27 smaller guns and, with a top speed of 22 knots, despite her 11-inch (279-mm) armour, she was the fastest battleship afloat. All other battleships were now obsolete, and the *Dreadnought* would give her name to a whole new class of battleship. Britain had, once again, taken the lead in the race for naval supremacy – and had no intention of relinquishing it.

HMS DREADNOUGHT

LAID DOWN	1905	**ARMAMENT**	10 x 12-in (305-mm) guns
LAUNCHED	1906		27 secondary guns
DISPLACEMENT	18,420 tons		5 x 18-in (457 mm) torpedo tubes
LENGTH	527 ft / 160 m		
BEAM	82 ft / 25 m		
DRAUGHT	26½ ft / 8 m		
SPEED	22 knots max		
CREW	695–773		

The completion of HMS *Dreadnought* heralded an entirely new age of naval warfare.

WHAT HAPPENED

From 1907 until 1912, HMS *Dreadnought* was the flagship of the Home Fleet. At the start of the First World War she was the flagship of the Fourth Battle Squadron in the North Sea, based at Scapa Flow. In March 1915 she became the only battleship to ram and sink a German submarine (the U-29).

In 1916 the *Dreadnought* was refitted and became the flagship of the Third Battle Squadron, based at Sheerness. She became flagship of the Fourth Battle Squadron again in March 1918, but was paid off in July. She was sold for scrap in 1921 for £44,000.

THE ORDNANCE QF 13-POUNDER

BACKGROUND

The Ordnance Quick Firing 13-Pounder Field Gun was standard issue for the British Royal Horse Artillery at the outbreak of the First World War. It fired the first British artillery round of the war on the Western Front at Bray, 10 miles (16 km) south-east of Mons, on 22 August 1914.

It entered service with the British army in 1904, superseding the Erhard QF 15-pounder (6.81 kg) and BL 12-pounder (5.45 kg) 6-hundredweight weapons, having been specifically designed in response to the lessons learnt between 1899 and 1902 in the Second Boer War.

THE WEAPON

As a 'galloping gun' drawn by six horses on a wheeled pole trail, the 3-inch (76-mm) calibre, 13-pounder (5.9 kg) had a maximum range of 5,900 yards (5,395 m). The Mark I, which had a wire wound barrel, was improved on by the Mark II, which had a tapered inner tube pressed into the outer tube.

The gun was originally intended to support fast-moving cavalry in the field, but in the First World War this function was largely obviated by the static nature of trench warfare.

73

Nevertheless the shrapnel or high-explosive rounds proved devastatingly effective against advancing infantry.

Against entrenched enemy positions, however, the 18-pounder (8.17 kg) weapon was far more effective, and the 13-pounders were eventually converted to high-angle mounts and deployed as anti-aircraft guns.

WHAT HAPPENED

Perhaps the QF 13-pounder's finest hour was covering the retreat of the British Expeditionary Force at the Battle of Le Cateau in August 1914. But they were also present at the Battles of Mons, the Marne, Ypres, Neuve Chapelle, Loos, the Somme, Avros and Cambrai. During the First World War the QF 13-pounder fired over 1,500,000 rounds on the Western Front alone.

The gun still remains in ceremonial service today, used for saluting by the King's Troop of the Royal Horse Artillery.

Saluting, the firing of ammunition and thus rendering oneself unarmed, is the equivalent of baring the head, offering an empty right hand, dropping the point of a sword or reversing arms. A visiting foreign warship would fire off all its guns on entering a foreign port to demonstrate that the guns were unloaded and thus it was incapable of attack.

Though robust and reliable, the ordnance QF 13-pounder was eventually to prove too small for the 'trench-busting' required in the First World War.

The 21-gun Royal Salute originates from the number seven. Seven was the standard number of guns on a warship in the 17th century. A ship would empty its seven guns to demonstrate its friendly intent. Shore batteries, having more guns and available dry gunpowder, customarily fired three to each shot fired by the entering ship, i.e. 21 guns. With the improvement in naval gunpowder manufacture and storage, gun for gun salutes were adopted, with land guns following suit.

The basic Royal Salute in Britain is 21 rounds, an extra 20 rounds added if the salute is given in a royal palace or park.

The Tower of London holds the record for the most rounds fired in a salute – 124. Whenever the Duke of Edinburgh's birthday happens to coincide with the Queen's official birthday, 124 rounds are fired: 21 for the Duke of Edinburgh, 20 for a royal palace, 21 for the City of London, 21 for the Queen, another 20 for a royal palace and another 21 for the City of London.

MONITORS AND 'Q' SHIPS

BACKGROUND

The Royal Navy has always had its fair share of unusual and quirky ships, often adapted to fulfil specific urgent requirements from the materials to hand, or created for experimental new weapons or strategies that were abandoned, the vessels then being used in roles for which they were never built. At the outbreak of the First World War in 1914 the 'Monitors' and 'Q' Ships were two such examples.

THE WEAPON

It was the Brazilian navy that came up with the idea for the British Monitors of the First World War, which were effectively floating armoured guns, very low in the water, designed for shelling enemy positions, or sneaking up to much larger enemy battleships, maybe even in harbour, and blasting them out of the water. They themselves had been inspired by developments during the American Civil War.

Several officers of the Southern Confederacy's navy had been impressed by the new ironclads being built in France and England. Their superiors would not allow them the

With shallow draft, huge guns and because they were extraordinarily low in the water, the Royal Navy Monitors were hard to hit, nimble and deadly.

time or the money to design or construct their own from scratch, but they were reluctantly permitted to do what they could with the sunken Union craft rotting on the banks of the James River in Virginia. Accordingly, they refloated a steam frigate named the *Merrimac*, cut her down to 2 feet (0.6 m) from the waterline and clad her with iron, so she looked like an upturned bath. A 7-inch (178-mm) gun protruded at either end, and she was given five guns on each broadside and a reinforced ram. On 8 March 1862, this new Confederate weapon steamed out to try her luck against the Union ships blockading the harbour. Before nightfall, she had sunk the 30-gun *Cumberland* and forced the 50-gun *Congress* to surrender, and had coolly moved on to engage the *Minnesota*. When it grew dark, she serenely puffed back to base, having exceeded the wildest hopes of the Southerners. They looked forward to finishing what they had started the following day.

But the Northerners had spent more time and money on their own mini-ironclad: the *Monitor*, effectively a floating armoured turret, with two 11-inch (279 mm) guns, which could be revolved by steam engine through 360 degrees to bring the guns to bear on anything.

The smaller guns of the *Merrimac* made no impact on the *Monitor*'s armour, and the Union ship, carrying less weight with its fewer guns, was too nimble and quick to be rammed. Darting round her adversary, the *Monitor* repeatedly fired into the weakening Southern ship from less than 100 yards (90 m). After three final shells perforated her coat of iron, the *Merrimac* turned tail and ran.

It was the victorious *Monitor* that the Brazilian navy was hoping to emulate, with three modern equivalents under construction in England. At the outbreak of the First World War, however, they were requisitioned by the Admiralty, who then realised how effective they were and had more constructed within the year. They carried 14-inch (356-mm) guns, a massive armament for their size; they had such a shallow draught that torpedoes simply slipped underneath them, and they were so low in the water that they were almost impossible for enemy gunners to hit.

THE ORIGINAL USS MONITOR

LAID DOWN	1861
LAUNCHED	1862
DISPLACEMENT	987 tons
LENGTH	172 ft / 52.4 m
BEAM	41 ft 6 in / 12.6 m
DRAUGHT	10 ft 6 in / 3.2 m
SPEED	8 knots
CREW	59
ARMAMENT	2 x 11-inch (279-mm) Dahlgren smooth-bores

HMS RAGLAN
(one of the original British First World War Monitors)

IN SERVICE	1915–18*
DISPLACEMENT	6,150 tons
LENGTH	320 ft / 97.5 m
BEAM	90 ft / 27.4 m
ARMAMENT	2 x 14-in (356-mm) guns
	2 x 6-in (152-mm) guns
	2 x 12-pdr (5.45-kg) guns

* She was sunk with another Monitor, the HMS *M28*, off Imbros by the Turkish battle-cruiser *Yavuz Sultan Selim*

The most effective of all the German weapons of attack on the sea in the First World War was the dreaded U-boat (Unterseeboot). Within two months of the declaration of war, three of the Royal Navy's light cruisers had been sunk within 58 minutes by a single U-boat.

To counter this threat, the convoy system, first developed by the Romans, copied by the British in the Middle Ages, and then again by Cromwell's 'wafters' – who were said to 'waft English shipping home' – was speedily reimposed.

The convoy system played an essential role during both World Wars in keeping Britain's overcrowded islands fed and her munitions factories running. Ever since the Napoleonic Wars, however, the Royal Navy had also had a tradition of decoy or 'Q' ships, which pretended to be helpless merchantmen, luring enemy warships up close before raising the white ensign, casting off their disguises and blasting them out of the water. One British frigate of the early 19th century took several French ships in succession by a series of double bluffs. It hung sail cloth badly painted with chequered gunports over her real gunports. When French ships raced up thinking they had detected a fake, the painted sailcloth was dropped away to reveal 32 real 24-pounder (10.89 kg) guns. It took two French privateers in this way and sank a French frigate.

WHAT HAPPENED

The First World War 'Q' ships, 'made up' to look like harmless colliers or sailing boats, followed in these heroic footsteps. On being attacked by a U-boat, they would often dispatch 'panic parties' of seamen in lifeboats, occasionally even dressed as women and children, to encourage the approaching U-boat to believe the 'merchantman' was abandoning ship. When the submarine came in for the kill, fake sides fell away to reveal guns far larger than those of any U-boat. They had no choice but to yield or be sunk.

THE AIRCRAFT CARRIER, or FLAT TOP

BACKGROUND

After the American Wright Brothers accomplished the first manned, powered flight in 1903, aircraft technology raced ahead in leaps and bounds. By 1910 the US Navy had succeeded in launching aircraft from the deck of a ship. It was Commander Charles Samson of the Royal Navy, however, who in May 1912 became the first person to take off from a moving warship. In a short S27 he flew off HMS *Hibernia* while she steamed at 10½ knots at the Royal Fleet Review at Weymouth. The following year the Royal Navy fitted out an aircraft carrier, effectively adding a flight deck to an old cruiser, HMS *Hermes*.

By the outbreak of the First World War, several more ships had been converted into aircraft carriers, including the old Cunard liner Campania, which carried 10 seaplanes.

THE WEAPON

HMS *Ark Royal* was the first vessel of the Royal Navy to be originally finished as an aircraft carrier. Even she was converted to that role while actually under construction, having previously been destined to become a 'tramp steamer'.

Originally cobbled together from whatever ships and parts lay to hand, the unwieldy 'flat tops' were to become the most powerful instruments of war on Earth.

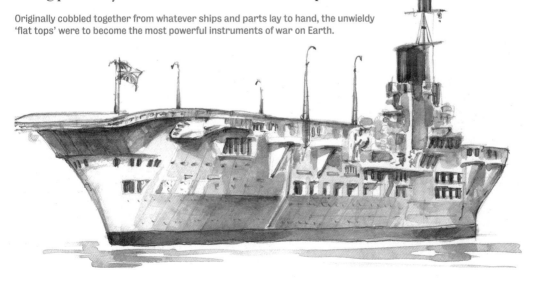

Her engines were moved back, and a flight deck was built over the front half of the ship. She was given an aircraft hold 150 feet (46 m) long, 45 feet (13.7 m) wide and 15 feet (4.6 m) high. Two 3-ton cranes were added, for lifting seaplanes through a sliding hatch on to the flight deck or down on to the sea.

Her five seaplanes took off over the bow and landed on water on their floats, to be retrieved by crane. Her two normal aeroplanes could only come down on land, having taken off at sea.

The Ark Royal spent the war in the Mediterranean and took part in the Gallipoli campaign in the Dardanelles.

HMS ARK ROYAL (renamed *Pegasus* in 1934)			
LAID DOWN	1913	**SPEED**	11 knots / 20 kph
LAUNCHED	1914	**CREW**	180
DISPLACEMENT	7,450 tons (loaded)	**ARMAMENT**	4 x 12-pdr (5.45 kg) guns
LENGTH	366 ft / 111.6 m		2 x .303-in (7.7-mm) Maxims
BEAM	50 ft 8 in / 15.5 m	**AIRCRAFT**	5 float planes
DRAUGHT	18 ft / 5.6 m		2 land planes

WHAT HAPPENED

Throughout the First World War, fear of meeting 'the great adversary', Britain's Royal Navy, confined the German High Seas Fleet to harbour. It was only in May 1916 that the British Grand Fleet and the German High Seas Fleet confronted each other in the Battle of Jutland.

The German Admiral von Scheer attempted to stage an ambush by bombarding the British coast with his battle-cruisers. This, he hoped, would entice the British Admiral Beatty to come out with his own battle-cruisers, at which point von Scheer's much larger battleships, waiting just over the horizon, would storm in and wreak carnage on the smaller British battle-cruisers before Admiral Jellicoe could dash down from Scapa Flow in Scotland to help them. Battleships were much more powerful than battle-cruisers.

But the British were forewarned by naval intelligence and Admiral Scheer's fleet of 22 battleships, 5 battle-cruisers, 10 light cruisers and 61 destroyers was, in fact, faced with a

British force of 28 battleships, 9 battle-cruisers, 8 armoured cruisers, 78 destroyers and 1 seaplane carrier: HMS *Engadine*.

Flight Lieutenant Rutland was the first British pilot to launch a carrier-based aircraft into battle. At one point, flying below 1,000 feet (305 m) in a seaplane, he attracted the fire of three cruisers and five destroyers. He escaped unscathed to report enemy positions back to his commanders on HMS *Engadine*.

At Jutland the British losses were worse than the Germans', famously prompting Admiral Beatty to demand, 'What's wrong with our bloody ships today?' But the German navy never dared risk battle again.

It was in the Second World War that Aircraft Carriers really came into their own, launching bombers into attack. At the Battle of Taranto in November 1940 the carrier-based British Fleet Airarm sank three mighty Italian battleships and a cruiser. In December 1941 carrier-based Japanese bombers destroyed the American Pacific Fleet based at Pearl Harbour in Hawaii. The Americans delivered their own knock-out counter punch at the Battle of Midway in June 1942, the bombers from US Carriers sinking all four Japanese carriers. The Aircraft Carrier had come of age.

THE LEWIS GUN

BACKGROUND

The Lewis gun, properly called the Lewis Automatic Machine Rifle, was invented by the US Army Colonel Isaac Newton Lewis in 1911, but it was not taken up by the American armed forces until it had proved its worth with the British.

In fact the Lewis gun was first used by the Belgian army at the outbreak of the First World War, and was known as the 'Belgian Rattlesnake' when it was quickly adopted by the British. With its broad, pipe-like barrel casing and top-mounted pan magazines, it had a very distinctive look and remained in use with British forces until the end of the Second World War.

It was often used as a vehicle-mounted machine gun and is alleged to be the first machine gun fired from an aeroplane.

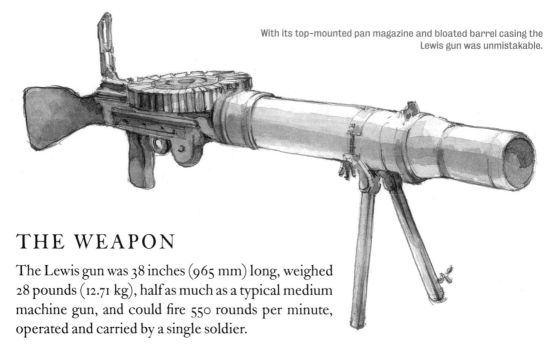

With its top-mounted pan magazine and bloated barrel casing the Lewis gun was unmistakable.

THE WEAPON

The Lewis gun was 38 inches (965 mm) long, weighed 28 pounds (12.71 kg), half as much as a typical medium machine gun, and could fire 550 rounds per minute, operated and carried by a single soldier.

As well as being only half as heavy as a normal contemporary machine gun, the Lewis consisted of only 62 parts, making it comparatively cheap and easy to mass-produce, of crucial importance in the First World War. Famously, six Lewis guns could be produced in the time it took to make one Vickers, at one sixth of the cost.

The design of the Lewis gun exploited the expanding gas produced by firing a bullet to eject the spent cartridge, load and fire the next.

It could take a 47-round drum magazine for infantry or 97-round drum magazine for use on aircraft.

WHAT HAPPENED

The British army took up the Lewis gun in late 1914. Normally, two men were responsible for the gun, one to carry ammunition and reload and one to fire, but in units with a Lewis every member was trained in its use, in case either of the two-man team was wounded.

The Lewis was mounted on British tanks and aircraft, though it proved impossible to synchronise with the propeller and therefore always had to be situated outside the propeller's arc.

When the Second World War broke out, the Lewis was replaced with the Bren gun where possible, but continued in service as a vehicle-mounted weapon throughout the war.

THE BRODIE TIN HAT

BACKGROUND

At the start of the First World War, none of the armies provided their soldiers with 'tin hats', and accordingly they suffered terrible head wounds, principally from shrapnel. The French introduced a steel helmet in the summer of 1915, the model 19/5 Adrian Helmet with a distinctive 'crown ridge', designed by Auguste-Louis Adrian. This was quickly adopted by the Belgian and Italian armies.

The British War Office rejected the Adrian design, because of the expense, the difficulties that mass production would pose, and the very limited protection it provided. Instead, they opted for a much stronger design by John L. Brodie, which could be pressed from a single sheet of steel. Even the British design, however, would not stop a bullet.

The Brodie first saw action at the Battle of St Eloi in April 1916. The Americans bought 400,000 when they entered the war in 1917 and the following year began to produce them in the United States.

THE WEAPON

The shallow, circular design with its leather liner and chinstrap offered good protection from above but left the neck exposed.

Brodie's initial design, the Type A, had a 2-inch (50-mm) brim and a shallow dome. It was soon replaced by the manganese steel Type B design with a deeper dome and smaller brim. The non-reflective finish was achieved with pulverised cork or sawdust. In 1917 a

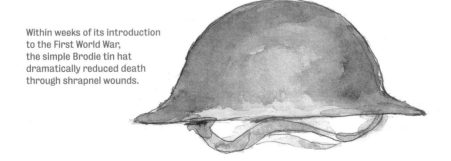

Within weeks of its introduction to the First World War, the simple Brodie tin hat dramatically reduced death through shrapnel wounds.

rubber cushion was added around the screw that held the liner in place at the top of the crown, but with few modifications the Brodie helmet continued in service with Britain's police, fire brigades, air-raid wardens and military until 1944.

WHAT HAPPENED

In 1944 the Mark III Turtle Helmet was introduced, and gradually superseded the Brodie. After the Falklands, Britain replaced steel helmets with synthetic Kevlar, which is light, strong and heat resistant, but the 'Brodie tin hat' is still used by the soldiers of a number of Commonwealth countries today.

THE SOPWITH CAMEL

BACKGROUND

Designed by Thomas Sopwith and built by his Sopwith Aviation Company, the Sopwith Camel was first issued to No. 70 Squadron of the Royal Flying Corps on the Western Front in July 1917. The Sopwith Camel was instantly recognised as a superb fighting machine, and the 5,490 eventually produced were to account for at least 3,000 enemy aircraft.

THE WEAPON

A one-man scouting plane, it was normally equipped with two forward-firing Vickers machine guns and four 25-pound (11.35-kg) bombs. It was the 'hump' enclosing the breeches of the twin Vickers guns that caused it to be named the Camel. Its single engine could take it up to speeds of 115 mph (185 kph), enabling it to reach a ceiling of 19,000 feet (5,800 m).

Although the Camel was much applauded and admired, the word 'vicious' was also frequently applied to it. It was tail-heavy, the slightest problem with fuel mix could lead to engine cut-out on take-off, and any stalling immediately resulted in a spin. Inexperienced or learner pilots, used to flying much easier planes, dreaded it. Nevertheless, it was sensitive and incredibly agile for its time and, most important of all, hugely successful in combat, winning back the skies from the German Albatross scouts.

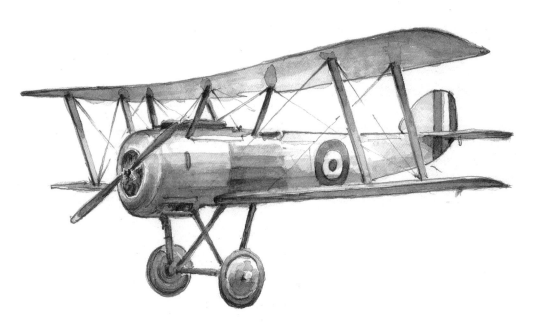

Despite its fragile appearance the Sopwith Camel was more than a match for the German Albatross Scouts.

The final production Camel 2 F.1 was specifically adapted for work at sea, and as well as being flown from aircraft-carriers, it could be catapulted from platforms on the forecastles or gun turrets of large ships, or launched from a lighter towed behind a destroyer. It was used with particular success when flown from HMS *Furious* and HMS *Pegasus*.

SOPWITH CAMEL F.1

TYPE	Biplane scout/fighter	**WEIGHT**	1,453 lb / 659 kg (loaded)
CREW	1	**HEIGHT**	8 ft 6 in / 2.59 m
POWER	One 130 hp Clerget rotary engine	**NUMBER BUILT**	5,490
SPEED	115 mph / 185 kph	**IN SERVICE**	1916–19
FLIGHT HEIGHT	19,000 ft / 5,790 m	**ARMAMENT**	2 x fixed forward-firing Vickers machine guns.
RANGE	(2½ hours) 300 miles / 485 km		4 x 25-lb (11.35-kg) bombs
WINGSPAN	28 ft / 8.53 m		
LENGTH	18 ft 9 in / 5.72 m		

WHAT HAPPENED

By the summer of 1918, the speed and height limitations of the Camel – it operated best below 12,000 feet (3,700 m) and never exceeded a speed of 120 mph (193 kph) – meant it was being superseded by faster fighters, and it was gradually relegated to ground attack and infantry support roles.

Only seven genuine Camels remain in flying condition.

FIRST WORLD WAR FIGHTER ACES
MANFRED VON RICHTHOFEN, 'The Red Baron' (Germany) – 80 'kills'
RENÉ PAUL FONCK (France) – 75
WILLIAM BISHOP (Canada) – 72
RAYMOND COLLISHAW (Canada) – 62
ERNST UDET (Germany) – 62
EDWARD MANNOCK (UK) – 61

THE TANK

BACKGROUND

Perhaps it is appropriate that Britain, the home of the last great European war chariot, should have invented the next tactical unit of wheeled force – the tank. Perhaps, too, it was inevitable that the home of the Industrial Revolution should be the first to harness mechanical power and mass-produce metal plate for military uses.

As early as the Crimean War, after seeing the gallant but catastrophic Charge of the British Light Brigade in 1855, an Englishman suggested protecting the driver of one of the new steam traction engines with an armoured cover, fitting big scythes to the wheel hubs and simply 'mowing down' opposing cavalry and infantry. Although his idea was dismissed as 'barbaric', the War Office did purchase traction engines with 'footed wheels', a predecessor of tracks, to tow guns at Woolwich Arsenal.

In the American Civil War the Confederates armed a steam tractor with a muzzle-loaded gun and protected it with steel plate. It was quickly captured at Harpers Ferry, West Virginia, and converted back to a tractor.

During the Boer War the Fowler Company produced four steam vehicles protected by boiler plate which could each tow up to four armoured wagons. Each wagon could accommodate 30 men or a field gun, and the system was enormously effective in warding off attacks by the Boer commandos.

The internal combustion engine provided more flexible alternatives. Frederick Simms's 'Motorised Quadricycle Shielded Maxim Gun Carrier', or 'Motor Scout', appeared in 1898. Four years later his 28-foot long, six-ton 'War Car' received massive publicity in the British press. It carried two machine guns and a quick-fire pom-pom gun encased in heavy armour. However, despite being hailed by the newspapers as 'the peacemaker' in 1902, it was not taken up by the War Office. Other 'war cars' did emerge in both Germany and France in 1904, with traversable or rotating turrets, but were still no more than modified passenger cars. It was not until 1908 that Armstrong Whitworth's purpose-built 40-horsepower armoured car appeared.

The Italians were the first to use armoured cars in combat, during the Italian-Turkish War in North Africa in 1912. The crude but reliable 35-horsepower vehicle was based on a long car chassis with a hand-traversed machine gun turret and was highly successful.

At the beginning of the First World War, after the planned German dash for Paris had ground to a halt, fighting on the Western Front became virtually static. The weapon of defence, the machine gun, had overtaken the weapon of attack, the rifle, and the war congealed into lines of fortified trenches, barbed wire, craters, mud, shellfire and spasms of heroically brave but often tragically ineffective infantry assaults. It was a deadly stalemate, and the finest military minds on both sides racked their brains to find some way to end it. Eventually it was the British tank that broke this lethal deadlock.

By a strange twist of fate, it was not the land forces of the British Empire that came up with the breakthrough but those of the sea and air – the Royal Navy Air Service. The First Lord of the Admiralty, Winston Churchill, ordered that 100 of what he then considered to be the finest British car, the Rolls-Royce, be fitted with armour and guns for use in patrol work and pilot rescue around the Royal Navy airstrips defending the European North Sea ports. There were not enough men available to patrol on foot. Accordingly, the Rolls-Royce Admiralty Turreted Pattern Armoured Car was created. This had a manually operated central turret, and it was eventually used in every theatre of the First World War, remaining in service until the 1930s. Such was its success that for a few months in 1915 a number of far heavier armoured vehicles, around 10 tons, were constructed, based on the American Seabrook Lorry Chassis with four Maxim machine guns and a 3-pounder (1.36 kg) naval gun. Their weight meant they were only truly effective on very hard, dry ground or roads, and production stopped almost as soon as it had begun.

Belgium patrol forces adapted some Minerva Touring Cars to ape the Rolls-Royce, and the Germans soon followed suit. The most numerous of all the armoured cars in use in the First World War was the Austin. It was originally ordered by the Russian Government, but was soon taken up by the British and other Allied armies.

THE WEAPON

Meanwhile, Captain Sueter of the Royal Navy Air Service, having been impressed by the armoured car, was developing the tank. He identified three crucial requirements. In the first place it had to be a 'shield on wheels' to protect advancing infantry from machine gun fire. Secondly, it needed to have wheels that could cope with the 'infernal mud'. Thirdly, it should be a 'trench-crosser', if at all possible.

Initial ideas revolved around enormous wheels, 45 feet (13.7 m) in diameter, to simply roll over the trenches, but these were deemed too easy a target for opposing artillery. Sueter then hit on the idea of 'endless tracks', like the rubber variety already produced by Diplock of London, known as Pedrails. Two Pedrail tracks, driven by separate engines, would be incorporated into a 'landship', with an armoured body, a 12-pounder (5.45 kg) naval gun and an eight-man crew. Colonel E.D. Swinton, an army staff officer based in France, was also exploring ideas along similar lines. Accordingly, Churchill set up the 'Landships Committee' in February 1915 to push the issue forward. In July 1915 the Committee asked Sir William Tritton of Fosters Engineers in Lincoln, to design and construct a working prototype. Working with armoured car designer Major W.G. Wilson, they produced the No. 1 Lincoln machine. Known as the 'Little Willie' – after William Tritton, W.G. Wilson and the German Crown Prince – this was the first practical tank. It had an armoured body, tracks, wheels on a rear trolley-like extension for steering, and a 2-pounder (0.91 kg) gun in a rotating turret.

Although it was certainly a mobile shield capable of coping with the 'infernal mud', it was seriously unstable on uneven ground and had not overcome the problem of trench-crossing. The War Office demanded that any landship must be able to cross a 9-foot (2.7- m) trench. Undeterred, Wilson and Tritton perfected a second prototype, which was not only more stable but could do just that – 'Big Willie'.

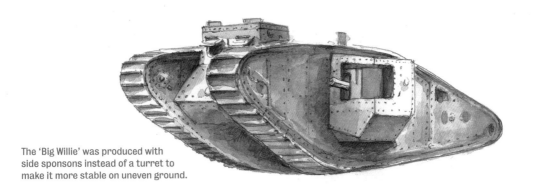

The 'Big Willie' was produced with side sponsons instead of a turret to make it more stable on uneven ground.

The structure of the hull was based on the 'Little Willie' prototype. They overcame Little Willie's instability by replacing the central top turret with two side turrets or 'sponsons', to lower the centre of gravity, and by bringing the tracks right up to the roof line of the vehicle, which resulted in the classic 'squashed oblong' or 'lozenge' shape.

Inside, the gearsmen and brakesmen flanked the central Daimler engine, responding to hand signals from the driver up ahead. A separate wheeled steering tail was added to increase stability and act as a rudder on wide turns. Tight turns were made by simply braking either track. Speed was limited to that of the advancing infantrymen, 3.7 mph.

Although Lord Kitchener dismissed Big Willie as a 'mechanical toy', the War Office was so impressed by a demonstration in January 1916 that it ordered 100.

Secrecy was paramount, and it was decided that the name 'landship' would give away the nature of the new wonder-

THE MARK I TANK BIG WILLIE

PRODUCED	1915–19
WEIGHT	Male: 28 tons Female: 27.4 tons
LENGTH	32 ft 6 in / 9.94 m
HEIGHT	8 ft / 2.44 m
CREW	8
ARMOUR	0.23–0.47 in / 6–12 mm
ENGINE	Foster-Daimler petrol engine 105 hp
SPEED	4 mph (6.4 kph) max
ARMAMENT	Male: 2 x 6-pdr (2.72 kg) QF guns Female: 4 x .303-in (7.7-mm) Vickers machine guns
SECONDARY	Male: 4 x .303-in (7.7-mm) Hotchkiss machine guns Female: 2 x .303-in (7.7-mm) Hotchkiss machine guns

weapon, were the enemy ever to hear of it while it was in production. The 'product' was accordingly referred to as 'mobile watertanks' – quickly abbreviated in official correspondence to 'tanks'. 'Big Willie' was the first tank ever to be deployed on the battlefield.

One of the very first military advocates of tracked shields, Colonel Swinton, was given command of the new 'heavy branch of the Motor Machine-Gun Corps', the first unit in the world to be issued with tanks. They first saw action at Flers, about 25 miles (40 km) west of Arras, on 15 September 1916, towards the end of the Somme offensive. Success there led to increased orders for the progressively improving models. The Mark IV entered service in February 1917.

The steering tail was abandoned. Originally, it was envisaged that 'female' tanks, armed with machine guns in their sponsons, would support 'male' tanks armed with 6-pounder naval guns in their sponsons, and indeed 'male', 'female' and 'hermaphrodite' tanks, a mixture of both, were produced. The Mark IV had smaller sponsons flush with the sides of the tank.

The 150 horsepower Mark V of 1915 was advanced enough for the driver to control the vehicle single-handed without having to relay his instructions back to gearsmen or brakesmen through hand signals. It had wider tracks, thicker armour and pop-up semaphore arms for communicating across the battlefield. The Mark V* was lengthened, enabling it to tackle even wider trenches.

WHAT HAPPENED

On 20 November 1917, at the Battle of Cambrai, almost every British tank in existence joined in a mass attack of 450 vehicles over a 6-mile (9.6-km) stretch of line, followed closely by five infantry divisions. The tanks at Cambrai carried bundles of brush and wood to drop into trenches to allow them to pass across. Meanwhile, old Mark Is, stripped of their guns, were equipped as mobile offices with wireless to act as command centres. Others were converted into supply tanks, following behind with equipment and ammunition.

They advanced 5 miles (8 km), exceeding almost every earlier offensive using artillery and infantry alone. The tank had secured its place on the battlefield.

THE MEDIUM TANK MARK A, or WHIPPET

BACKGROUND

The Big Willies of the First World War were designed to shield advancing infantry and penetrate the enemy lines by crossing the trenches. Once they had proved their effectiveness, the War Office also saw a role for a lighter tank to exploit these breakthroughs as and when they had been achieved. Accordingly, in 1918, the Whippet was introduced to the battlefield.

THE WEAPON

The Medium Tank Mark A, initially named the Tritton Chaser but quickly retitled the Whippet, was powered by two London bus engines, one for each track, and armed with three Hotchkiss machine guns. It was half the weight of a Big Willie, carried a crew of three rather than eight, and could reach speeds of up to 9 mph (14.5 kph).

THE MEDIUM TANK MARK A, or WHIPPET			
PRODUCED	1917–18	**HEIGHT**	9 ft / 2.75 m
IN SERVICE	1918–30	**CREW**	3
WEIGHT	14 tons	**ARMOUR**	0.5 in / 14 mm
LENGTH	20 ft / 6.10 m	**SPEED**	8.3 mph / 13.4 kph
WIDTH	8 ft 7 in / 2.62 m	**ARMAMENT**	4 x .303-in (7.7-mm) Hotchkiss machine guns

WHAT HAPPENED

Whippets earned their spurs covering the retreat of the infantry divisions after the German Spring Offensive of 1918. Later seven Whippets routed two entire German infantry battalions, killing over 400 men.

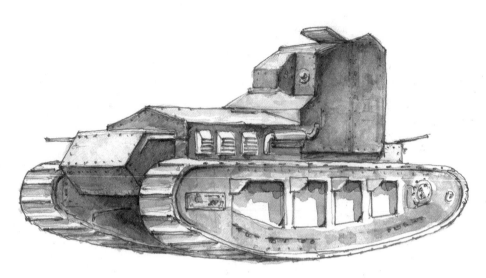

After the success of the Big Willies the British designed lighter tanks like the Whippet and the Hornet to exploit any breakthroughs achieved by their larger cousins.

Nearly 100 Whippets went into action at Amiens in August 1918 with great success, but they were left far behind by the horse cavalry as soon as they broke into rougher country. Never again would the British Army set out to use horses and tanks together. In the Amiens Offensive of August 1918, Whippets broke right through the German lines, capturing a great swathe of German artillery. One Whippet, 'Music Box', was cut off behind enemy lines for nine hours, during which it inflicted heavy casualties and destroyed an artillery battery, an observation balloon, an entire infantry camp and a transport column.

The Whippet had two drawbacks: steering was a constant battle between the two competing track engines, and the heat was often oppressive in the tiny driving space.

The Mark C, or Hornet, also designed by Tritton, was a larger machine with many improvements. It was intended for use in 'Plan 1919', the mass tank attack planned for the 1919 Spring Offensive that, thanks to the end of hostilities in 1918, never happened. However, the Hornet remained in service with the Tank Corps until 1936.

THE VICKERS MACHINE GUN

BACKGROUND

The Vickers machine gun evolved from the earlier Maxim gun. Vickers took over the Maxim Company in 1896 and, while improving the design of the original Maxim gun and adding a 'muzzle booster', managed to reduce the weight.

The new Vickers weapon became the standard heavy machine gun of the British army in 1912, and its reliability, durability and effectiveness in the First World War earned it the title 'Queen of the Battlefield'.

THE WEAPON

Depending on the different varieties of equipment used, a Vickers weighed between 25 and 30 pounds (11.35–13.62 kg), and its tripod between 40 and 50 pounds (18.16–22.70 kg). The 250-round cloth ammunition belts weighed 22 pounds (9.99 kg) in their boxes, and each gun needed a gallon (4.5 litres) of water for the water jacket fitted around the barrel to prevent overheating. Crucially for combat in hot climates, a rubber hose fed steam from the water jacket to a condensing bottle, which preserved precious water supplies in arid conditions.

The Vickers took the standard .303-inch (7.7-mm) British army rifle bullet and fired between 450 and 600 rounds per minute. It could kill at up to 4,500 yards (4,100 m), but its effective range was considered to be around 2,440 feet (744 m), beyond which it was no longer accurate.

The gun normally had a six-man crew, one to lead the crew and fire, one to feed the ammunition, and four to assist, though all six were fully trained in operating and maintaining the weapon.

WHAT HAPPENED

Before the outbreak of the First World War, Vickers were making 12 machine guns a week. At the outbreak of war in August 1914, they stepped up production dramatically, and were

The six-man crew of a single Vickers
Machine Gun could break the advance
of an entire German regiment.

charging the War Office £175 per gun. There was public outrage at what was regarded as 'war profiteering' – making money out of the slaughter. They reduced the price to £80. By 1918 they were shipping just under 760 guns a week.

From 1916 the Vickers was fitted as standard to French and British aircraft, with interrupter gears to allow it to fire through the arc of the spinning propeller and vents in the water jacket to allow for cooling by airflow.

While attacking High Wood during the Battle of the Somme in August 1916, the 100th Company of the Machine Gun Corps fired a million rounds from 10 Vickers machine guns non-stop for 12 hours, without a single jam or stoppage. Ten barrels were worn out by each gun, 100 in all. No barrel change took more than two minutes.

The Vickers was retired from service with the British Army in 1968, to be replaced by the L7 GPMG. It remains a reserve weapon with the armies of India, Pakistan and Nepal.

THE ROYAL AIRCRAFT FACTORY SE.5

BACKGROUND

The Royal Aircraft Factory SE.5 biplane (the SE stood for Scout Experimental) entered service with the Royal Flying Corps in March 1917. After a change to the over-large windscreen, it proved to be more than a match for the latest German fighters.

THE WEAPON

The comments of Sholto Douglas, who commanded a Royal Flying Corps squadron of SE.5s, help explain why the plane is now regarded as the Spitfire of the First World War. Douglas identified the following features:

- Comfortable with a good all-round view

- Retaining performance and manoeuvrability at height

- Steady and quick to gain speed in a dive

- Capable of a very fine zoom

- Useful in both offence and defence

- Strong in design and construction

- Reliable engine

The SE.5's famous high-speed dive (without breaking up!) was particularly valued; indeed, with its top speed of 138 mph (222 kph) it was one of the fastest aircraft of the First World War. It also provided a stable gun platform and, although less nimble than a Sopwith Camel, was relatively manoeuvrable, and much easier and safer to fly.

It had one synchronised .303-inch (7.7-mm) Vickers machine gun, unlike the Camel, which had two, but the additional wing-mounted Lewis gun allowed the pilot to fire at aircraft below. Its great advantage over the Camel was its exemplary performance at height, allowing it to compete with the German Fokker D.VII.

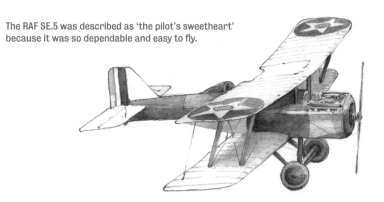

The RAF SE.5 was described as 'the pilot's sweetheart' because it was so dependable and easy to fly.

THE ROYAL AIRCRAFT FACTORY SE.5

TYPE	Biplane fighter/scout
CREW	1
POWER	One 200 hp Wolseley-built 8-cylinder Hispano-Suiza 8a V-type
SPEED	138 mph / 222 kph
FLIGHT HEIGHT	17,000 ft / 5,185 m
RANGE	300 miles / 483 km
WINGSPAN	26 ft 7 in / 8.11 m
WEIGHT	1,988 lb / 902 kg
HEIGHT	9 ft 6 in / 2.89 m
NUMBER BUILT	5,265
IN SERVICE	1917–22
ARMAMENT	1 x fixed forward-firing .303 (7.7-mm) Vickers machine gun 1 x .303 (7.7-mm) Lewis gun on upper wing

WHAT HAPPENED

The legendary ace, James McCudden, wrote of the Royal Aircraft SE.5: 'It was very fine to be in a machine that was faster than the Huns, and to know that one could run away just as things got too hot.' Nevertheless, problems in engine supply restricted the number put into service. By 1918 nearly 3,000 were in operation, having served with 24 British, one Australian and two American squadrons.

THE MILLS BOMB

BACKGROUND

For most of us the word grenade conjures the image of the classic Mills pineapple design: a segmented, fist-sized lump of cast iron, with an activating lever held in place with a pin.

The Mills bomb was used by the British army for 60 years – from May 1915 until June 1975 – and at least 70 million were made, as well as numerous copies.

William Mills, a golf-club designer from Sunderland, who had trained as a marine engineer, introduced and manufactured the 'Mills bomb' at his 'Mills Munition Factory' in Birmingham at the outbreak of the First World War.

THE WEAPON

Designated as the No. 5, it was adopted by the British army in 1915. The grenade was 3¾ in (95 mm) long and 2½ in (63 mm) wide, like an elongated cricket ball, but at 1½ pounds (0.68 kg) it was about five times heavier. It could be thrown about 30 yards (27 m) with a fair degree of accuracy. You pulled out the pin to activate the grenade before throwing it.

The pineapple effect was originally designed to help the thrower grip the grenade, but incidentally assisted fragmentation on explosion.

WHAT HAPPENED

The Mills bomb underwent a variety of modifications. The No. 23 had a tubular base plug that allowed it to be fired from a rifle – up to a distance of 150 yards (137 m). The No. 26, introduced in the 1930s, had a detachable base plate enabling it to be fired from a rifle discharger cup. Until the Second World War, the grenade had a seven-second fuse, but this was reduced to four seconds.

In 1972 the Mills bomb, by then the No. 36M Mark I, was discontinued by the British Army, but it remained in service with several Commonwealth armies until the late 1980s.

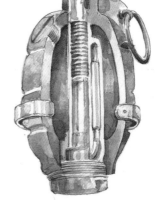

Simple to make and use and highly effective, the Mills Bomb won instant praise from the British Army and her allies as soon as it was introduced.

PART IV

THE SECOND WORLD WAR *and* BEYOND

THE FAIRBAIRN-SYKES FIGHTING KNIFE

BACKGROUND

The Fairbairn-Sykes Fighting Knife evolved during the 1930s in Shanghai and is still in use today. William Fairbairn, a former Royal Marine, was head of the Shanghai Municipal Police Riot Squad and set up the Shanghai Municipal Police Armoury.

Eric Sykes, who had been a marksman in the First World War, was a Shanghai estate agent who was also a police reserve sergeant in charge of Shanghai's volunteer police sniper unit.

Both had extensive encounters with the Shanghai underworld, where the use of the knife had been refined to an art. Fairbairn had also undergone extensive martial arts instruction and was a black belt in jiu-jitsu.

Both saw the need for a knife specifically designed for hand-to-hand fighting.

THE WEAPON

In his book *Get Tough*, Fairbairn describes the two most important attributes of any fighting knife: balance and keenness. The blade must not be too heavy, or it falls from the grip when loosely held. It must have a 'sharp stabbing point' and 'good cutting edges' – because a cut artery bleeds much more profusely than one merely torn. It is also essential that the knife be slim enough to slip easily between the ribs.

In due course he was to champion the left-handed draw, for surprise, and the stomach slash to disconcert one's opponent, 'however notional the wound'.

When considering blade length, Fairbairn and Sykes must have taken the 1924 report issued by the Small Arms School at Hythe into account.

The report concluded that a 6-inch blade was long enough to deal with the most heavily dressed potential enemies – specifically a Russian soldier in cold weather kit. It also recognised that a 'short handy weapon' will beat a 'long cumbersome weapon' handled by an equally skilled man almost every time.

Accordingly, the Fairbairn-Sykes Fighting Knife is straight-bladed and double-edged, with a blade between 6 and 7 ½ inches (150–190 mm) long, designed for thrusting and slashing. The stiletto, with which it is often compared, was only designed for stabbing. The Fairbairn-Sykes knife is roughly 12 inches (305 mm) long and weighs around 8 ounces (227 g).

The grip, normally 5 inches (130 mm) long, was originally made of brass and 'knurled' to assist a secure grasp. The point of balance was 1 inch (2.5 cm) down the grip from the guard. The 'vase-like cylindrical handle', like that on a rapier, is one of the most distinctive features of the Fairbairn-Sykes knife, allowing for minute control.

The weapon was originally made in the Shanghai Municipal Police Armoury from a stock of old bayonets. It was issued to the police for use against gangsters and sold to private buyers. US Marine officers seemed particularly appreciative.

At the outbreak of the Second World War, Fairbairn joined the Special Operations Executive (SOE) as a silent killing instructor, and Sykes the Special Training Centre, at Lochailort in Inverness-shire, as a knife instructor.

No close combat fighting knives were available in Britain in 1940, so Fairbairn persuaded the Wilkinson Sword Company to make 300 from old bayonets, but he had to guarantee their sale personally.

Such was the success of the knife that the first British government order was placed in January 1941, and before long not only the SOE but also the British Commandos, SAS and special forces across the world would use nothing else.

Originally made from converted bayonets the Fairbairn-Sykes fighting knife soon became the weapon of choice for special forces across the Globe.

WHAT HAPPENED

The Fairbairn-Sykes Fighting Knife saw military action in the Second World War, Korea and Vietnam, and its great effectiveness led to the production of a myriad of copies and imitations.

The memorial to the Commandos, in Westminster Abbey, includes a solid gold Fairbairn-Sykes Fighting Knife, placed there by the Queen.

THE FAIREY SWORDFISH, or 'STRINGBAG'

BACKGROUND

In the early 1930s, the Air Ministry had a need for a new spotter plane. The word 'spotting' coming from their original purpose of noting the fall of enemy gunfire. The Fairey Aviation Company responded by producing a large biplane with a fabric-cloaked metal frame and folding wings for storage on aircraft carriers – some also had floats for landing after launch from catapults.

The large size of the Fairey 'Swordfish' made it suitable for several roles, and although it entered service in 1936 as a fleet attack aircraft, it was also deployed as an anti-submarine and training craft. It was nicknamed 'Stringbag' after the housewives' string shopping bag that could 'carry anything'. There were 13 Royal Navy 'Stringbag' squadrons at the outbreak of war in 1939.

THE WEAPON

The speed of innovation and development in time of war meant that the Swordfish was in fact outdated almost as soon as it saw active service. Its maximum speed of 138 mph (222 kph) was comparatively slow, and the necessity of a long, straight approach at these speeds was deadly for pilots against heavily defended targets. Not a single Swordfish survived the attack on German battle-cruisers during the 'Channel Dash' of February 1942.

Despite their ramshackle appearance and lack of speed British Fairey Swordfish sank three battleships at the Battle of Taranto.

THE FAIREY SWORDFISH

TYPE	Torpedo, scout aircraft
CREW	3
POWER	One 820 hp Bristol Pegasus XXX radial engine
SPEED	138 mph (222 kph)
FLIGHT HEIGHT	19,250 ft / 5,867 m
RANGE	546 miles / 879 km
WINGSPAN	45 ft 6 in / 13.96 m
LENGTH	35 ft 8 in / 10.87 m
WEIGHT	7,510 lb / 3,406 kg (loaded)
HEIGHT	12 ft 4 in / 3.76 m
NUMBER BUILT	2,392
IN SERVICE	1936–45
ARMAMENT	1 x fixed forward-firing .303-in (7.7-mm) machine gun 1 x .303-in (7.7-m) trainable gun in rear cockpit 1 x 18-in (457-mm) torpedo or 8 x 60 lb (27.24 kg) rockets

WHAT HAPPENED

For all its faults, the necessities of war kept the Swordfish in service until the fall of Germany, and it achieved some staggering successes.

In November 1940, Swordfishes sank three Italian battleships and a cruiser at the Battle of Taranto. This, allegedly, inspired the Japanese to begin planning their own aircraft attack on Pearl Harbor.

It was a Swordfish from HMS *Ark Royal* that inflicted the crucial damage to the Bismarck's rudder that prevented the mammoth German battleship from escaping back to France. Within 13 hours it had been sunk.

The Swordfish were so slow that they often threw the German gunners' fire-control predictors into total confusion, making them miss, way in front, time after time.

In all, 2,392 Swordfish were built, mostly the Mark II version. The last Swordfish squadron was disbanded in August 1946.

THE SHORT SUNDERLAND, or 'FLYING PORCUPINE'

BACKGROUND

The Short Sunderland was a flying-boat patrol bomber that struck terror into the hearts of Nazi Germany's U-boat commanders and became one of the longest-serving British military aircraft, from the late 1930s to the late 1960s.

The 1930s were the heyday of the long-range passenger flying-boats, and the one made by Short Brothers of Rochester was so admired that the Air Ministry asked them to design a military version.

THE WEAPON

Borrowing heavily from its civilian forebear, the Short Sunderland had two decks, a galley, bunks, a machine shop for in-flight repairs and even a porcelain loo. It could take crews of up to 11. Portable beaching gear enabled the craft to be pulled up on shore, after landing on water. There were four engines on the wings and six drum fuel tanks, with a further four smaller tanks added later behind the rear-wing span to allow for patrols of up to 14 hours' duration.

The Short Sunderland military flying boats remained in use in regions without proper runways for decades after the Second World War.

The new military flying-boat had four machine guns in the tail turret, two in the bow turrets, two in the dorsal turrets and two fixed forward-firing guns. It could carry up to 5,000 pounds (2,270 kg) of depth charges, mines or bombs.

THE SHORT SUNDERLAND MK.V

TYPE	Long-range sea-boat
CREW	8–11
POWER	Four 1,200 hp Pratt & Whitney R-1830-90 Twin Wasp 14-cylinder air-cooled radial engines
SPEED	217 mph / 349 kph
FLIGHT HEIGHT	17,900 ft / 5,445 m
RANGE	2,980 miles / 4,797 km
WINGSPAN	112 ft 9 in / 34.36 m
LENGTH	85 ft 3 in / 26 m
WEIGHT	66,000 lb / 27,216 kg (loaded)
HEIGHT	32 ft 10½ in / 10 m
IN SERVICE	1938–67
ARMAMENT	Two fixed forward-firing .303-in (7.7-mm) machine guns, two more in the bow turrets, two in the dorsal turrets and four in the tail turret. Up to 5,000 lb (2,270 kg) of bombs, mines or depth charges

The design was considered so ideal that 21 were ordered by the Air Ministry before the first test flight.

WHAT HAPPENED

At the outbreak of the Second World War, two Sunderlands immediately proved their worth by rescuing the entire 34-man crew of a torpedoed merchantman – but the Sunderland could also bite. The craft's first single-handed U-boat kill was achieved in July 1940, but in April that year a Sunderland, attacked by six German Junker Ju88 medium bombers off

Norway, downed one, severely damaged another and fought off the rest. From then on it was known by the Luftwaffe as 'das Fliegende Stachelschwein' – the flying porcupine – for its extraordinary defensive capabilities and ferocious firepower.

Not only surprisingly hard to 'kill' by enemy fighters, Sunderlands could also carry far more than their official load. One reputedly evacuated over four times the designated load during the fall of Crete to the Germans in May 1941, and 10 were deployed in the 1948–9 Berlin Airlift.

It was a Short Sunderland that 'spotted' the Italian fleet at anchor in Taranto before the Battle of Taranto in November 1940 – a stunning victory for the Royal Navy's Fleet Air Arm.

The development of Torpex depth charges in 1943, that would sink to a specific depth before exploding, eliminated the earlier problems of 'bounce-back' in which bombs occasionally ricocheted back off the target and endangered the aircraft that had just dropped them.

At the end of the war the presumption was that military flying-boats were obsolete, and a number of new Sunderlands awaiting delivery were simply flown out to sea and scuttled. However, in regions where modern runways were scarce, such as the Far East, Sunderlands remained in service until the late 1960s.

THE HAWKER HURRICANE

BACKGROUND

Seven out of 10 of all the enemy aircraft shot down by Fighter Command during the Battle of Britain, from July to October 1940, were shot down by 1,720 Hawker Hurricanes. Developed from the Hawker Fury biplane, it was originally known as the Fury Monoplane. The first, renamed the Hawker Hurricane, was delivered to No.111 Squadron at Northolt in November 1937, a year before the Spitfire would enter service.

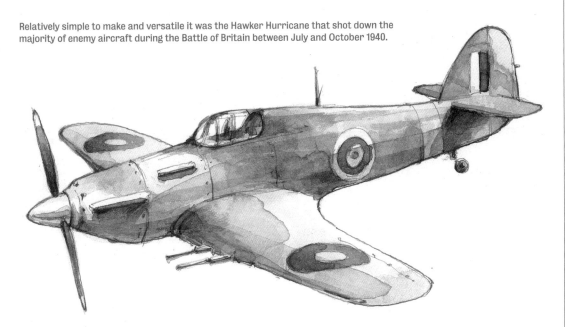

Relatively simple to make and versatile it was the Hawker Hurricane that shot down the majority of enemy aircraft during the Battle of Britain between July and October 1940.

THE WEAPON

Like the Spitfire, the Hurricane had an enclosed cockpit and retractable undercarriage, but the tubular metal structure with fabric covering could be produced much more quickly and simply than the difficult shapes and stressed skin of the Spitfire.

By September 1939, 18 Fighter Command squadrons were Hawker Hurricane, and despite the desperate need for fighters in Britain, the aeroplanes had also been exported to Turkey, Finland, Poland and Romania.

Within two years, Hurricanes were active in the Far East, and it was during the Burma campaign that the craft really showed what it could do in ground attack. But Hurricanes were nothing if not versatile.

Sea Hurricanes were deployed on 'CAM ships' (Catapult Aircraft Merchantmen), specially converted merchant ships, as early as 1941.

Some of those produced by the Canadian Car and Foundry Co. in Canada were fitted with fixed skis, which allowed them to take off and land on snow and ice. The Soviet Union took over 20 per cent of the total UK production of Hurricanes, nearly 3,000.

Over 13,000 were built in the UK by Hawker, Gloster & Austin Motors, and nearly 1,500 in Canada.

THE HAWKER HURRICANE MKIID (ANTI-TANK)

TYPE	Monoplane fighter
CREW	1
POWER	One 1,460 hp Rolls-Royce Merlin XX 12-cylinder V-type
SPEED	322 mph / 518 kph
FLIGHT HEIGHT	32,100 ft / 9,785 m
RANGE	900 miles / 1,448 km
WINGSPAN	40 ft / 12.19 m
LENGTH	32 ft 2 in / 9.81 m
WEIGHT	8,100 lb / 3,674 kg (loaded)
HEIGHT	13 ft 1 in / 3.98 m
NUMBER BUILT	14,531
IN SERVICE	1937–47
ARMAMENT	2 x fixed 1.58-in (40-mm) Vickers 's' guns under each wing
	2 x Browning .303-in (7.7-mm) machine guns in each wing

WHAT HAPPENED

The Hurricane was outclassed by both the Messerschmitt Bf 109 and the Spitfire, but it entered service earlier than the Spitfire, was simpler to produce and gave great and valiant service throughout the Second World War.

On 20 August 1940, Winston Churchill said of the pilots of the RAF:

THE GRATITUDE OF EVERY HOME IN OUR ISLAND, IN OUR EMPIRE, AND INDEED THROUGHOUT THE WORLD, EXCEPT IN THE ABODES OF THE GUILTY, GOES OUT TO THE BRITISH AIRMEN WHO, UNDAUNTED BY ODDS, UNWEARIED IN THEIR CONSTANT CHALLENGE AND MORTAL DANGER, ARE TURNING THE TIDE OF THE WORLD WAR BY THEIR PROWESS AND BY THEIR DEVOTION. NEVER IN THE FIELD OF HUMAN CONFLICT WAS SO MUCH OWED BY SO MANY TO SO FEW. ALL HEARTS GO OUT TO THE FIGHTER PILOTS, WHOSE BRILLIANT ACTIONS WE SEE WITH OUR OWN EYES DAY AFTER DAY.

THE SUPERMARINE SPITFIRE

BACKGROUND

The Spitfire and its arch-enemy the Messerschmitt Bf 109, are recognised as the finest fighter planes of the Second World War.

There were eventually to be 24 Marks of Spitfire, the first entering service with the RAF on 4 August 1938 with 19 Squadron. The first public outing for a Spitfire in RAF colours was on Empire Air Day at Duxford in May 1939, when the pilot 'belly-flopped' his aircraft, having forgotten to lower the newfangled undercarriage. He was fined five pounds by the Air Ministry.

The Spitfire was the only Allied fighter that continued to be produced throughout the war. A total of 20,351 were built, as well as 2,334 Seafires, the naval version. Some examples remained in service with air forces around the world until the mid 1960s.

THE WEAPON

The Spitfire was designed by R.J. Mitchell, the chief designer of the Supermarine Subsiduary of Vickers/Armstrongs. Mitchell was famously obsessed with streamlining, and it was the elliptical wing he developed, which allowed for higher top speeds than many of its contemporaries, that also gave the single-seat Spitfire its distinctive appearance.

Mitchell designed the Spitfire as a private venture, with the backing of Vickers/ Armstrongs, and included such high-tech innovations as a retractable undercarriage, an enclosed cockpit, oxygen breathing equipment and the newly developed Rolls-Royce PV/12 – the Merlin engine.

The Air Ministry suggested the name 'Shrew' for the new aircraft, intending to prompt an association with a woman of 'fiery temperament'. Sir Robert Maclean, chairman of Vickers/Armstrongs, preferred the old Elizabethan word 'Spitfire', which he used to describe his 'gutsy little spitfire' of a daughter, Anne. 'Just the sort of bloody silly name they would choose,' Mitchell mused philosophically.

THE SUPERMARINE SPITFIRE MKVB

TYPE	Fighter monoplane
CREW	1
POWER	One 1,440 hp Rolls-Royce Merlin 45/46/50 V-12 engine
SPEED	374 mph / 602 kph
FLIGHT HEIGHT	37,000 ft / 11,280 m
RANGE	470 miles / 756 km
WINGSPAN	36 ft 10 in / 11.23 m
LENGTH	29 ft 11 in / 9.11 m
WEIGHT	6,785 lb / 3,078 kg (loaded)
HEIGHT	11 ft 5 in / 3.48 m
NUMBER BUILT	20,351
IN SERVICE	1938–55
ARMAMENT	2 x .79-in (20-mm) cannon and 4 x .303 (7.7-mm) machine guns in wings

The Spitfire was more nimble, and had better visibility than the Messerschmitt Bf 109. There were initially problems with fuel cut-outs during steep dives, but the designer Beatrice Shilling came up with a metal diaphragm, known as Miss Shilling's Orifice, which cured the problem until fuel-injection was introduced in 1943.

WHAT HAPPENED

Although the Spitfire is often credited with winning the Battle of Britain, more Hawker Hurricanes saw action in the crucial stages of 1940, and the placement of the Hurricane's guns was then more effective, producing a closer pattern of fire. The Hurricane, however, had a lower speed and poorer performance at height than the Spitfire, so where possible the Hurricane squadrons took on the German bombers while the Spitfires engaged the fighter escorts. Seven out of every 10 German aircraft brought down during the Battle of Britain were destroyed by Hurricanes, but there were fewer Spitfires in the air and their kill ratio was marginally higher.

Obsessed with streamlining as he was, it was the designer RJ Mitchell's elliptical wing that gave the Spitfire its unmistakable profile.

After the Battle of Britain the Spitfire seemed to have the psychological edge. The Germans developed 'Spitfire complex', calling 'Achtung Schpitfeuer!' over their wireless to each other when they believed Spitfires to be in the vicinity. A grounded Canadian pilot in Malta, unable to take to the skies but armed with a ground radio set, induced such panic in German pilots with his bogus warnings in German of approaching Spitfires that two 109s shot each other down above his head. He was officially credited with two 'kills'.

The last Spitfires to be flown in combat were the Israeli and Egyptian Spitfires that fought each other in the Arab–Israeli War of 1948. They were officially retired from the RAF in 1955.

TOP SECOND WORLD WAR FIGHTER ACES

ERICH HARTMANN (Germany) - 352

HIROYOSHI NISHIZAWA (Japan) – 113

IVAN KOZHEDUB (USSR) – 62
(The USSR's Lydia Litvak was the top woman ace ever, with 12 kills.)

PIERRE CLOSTERMANN (France) – 33

TERESIO MARTINOLI (Italy) – 22

STANISLAW SKALSKI (Poland) – 22

SEVIN HEGLUND (Norway) – 14   *Continued. overleaf*

GERALD KESSELER (Holland) – 16

DEZSO SZENTGYORGI (Hungary) – 34

KAREL MIROSLAV KUTTELWASCHER (Czechoslovakia) – 20

MATO DUBOVAK (Croatia) – 40

CONSTANTINE CANTACUZINE (Romania) – 60

MARMADUKE 'PAT' PATTLE (South Africa) – 40+

JAMES 'JOHNNIE' JOHNSON (UK) – 36

BRENDAN 'PADDY' FINUCANE (Ireland) – 32

GEORGE BEURLING (Canada) – 31

CLIVE CALDWELL (Australia) – 28

COLIN GRAY (New Zealand) – 27

THE PIAT

BACKGROUND

At the outbreak of the Second World War in 1939, contemporary tanks were practically invulnerable to weapons carried by infantrymen. Britain's solution was the 'Projector, Infantry, Anti-Tank', or PIAT, which reached the battlefield in 1943, in time for the German invasion of Sicily.

THE WEAPON

This 39-inch (990-mm), 31-pound (14.07-kg), mortar-like weapon fired a high-explosive round with virtually no smoke or back blast, unlike the American bazooka. It was short, making it useful in close combat and house-to-house fighting, and could penetrate 4 inches (100 mm) of armour. However, the PIAT had a limited range, no more than 100 yards (91 m), and required considerable effort to cock (a 200-pound or 90-kg pull). If firing a round failed to reset the 'spigot', as it was supposed to do, the operator had either to lie on his back or stand up to re-cock it.

The 3-pound (1.36-kg) high-explosive round could penetrate the frontal armour of the most up-to-date German tanks, but only just, and then only with a direct hit, so practised hands preferred a shot at the side or rear armour.

PIAT rounds were notoriously 'nervy' and tended to explode if banged or dropped, and yet failed to fire if not perfectly positioned in the projector – necessitating lengthy and dangerous removal and re-cocking. Nevertheless, the PIAT could be devastating in a mortar-like role, clearing buildings or bunkers and against tanks.

Official instructions for priming and use of a PIAT from the 1943 British Army Manual read as follows:

LIE ON BACK AND REST PROJECTOR ON CHEST, WITH BOMB SUPPORT POINTING OVER ONE SHOULDER AND THE SHOULDER PIECE FLAT ON THE GROUND. KEEP THE FRONT SUPPORT CLEAR OF THE BODY AND ARMS. PLACE THE INSTEPS ON THE SHOULDER PIECE, ONE FOOT ON EACH SIDE OF THE OUTER CASING. GRASP THE TRIGGER GUARD FIRMLY WITH ONE HAND FROM UNDERNEATH; WITH THE OTHER GRASP ANY PART OF THE PROJECTOR THAT WILL GIVE GOOD LEVERAGE. SIT UP OR BEND THE KNEES IF NECESSARY, ACCORDING TO COVER. PULL THE OUTER CASING AWAY FROM THE SHOULDER PIECE AND TURN IT ANTI-CLOCKWISE AS FAR AS IT WILL GO. PULLING WITH THE HANDS AND PUSHING WITH THE FEET, CONTINUE TO PULL ON THE OUTER CASING UNTIL A CLICK IS HEARD. CONSIDERABLE EFFORT IS REQUIRED TO OVERCOME THE RESISTANCE OF THE MAINSPRING. THE CLICK DENOTES THE ACTION IS COCKED.

WHAT HAPPENED

On D-Day, 6 June 1944, having been dropped by glider to take and hold the vital Caen Canal Bridge, Sergeant Charles Thornton of the Oxfordshire and Buckinghamshire Light Infantry used his PIAT to block German forces on their way to the invasion beaches. Accompanied by Private Eric Woods, with one PIAT and only two rounds between them, lying totally exposed on the side of the road as two German half-tracks bore down on them, he blew up the leading vehicle. The burning half-track blocked the road and the Germans withdrew, believing the British to be armed with 6-pounder (2.72 kg) anti-tank guns.

The citation for Major Robert Cain's Victoria Cross at Arnhem in September 1944 describes how, armed with a PIAT, he put four Tiger tanks out of action, as well as two smaller tanks and three self-propelled guns.

In 1950 the British Army retired the PIAT from service in favour of the American M20 Super-Bazooka.

THE HOME GUARD, or 'DAD'S ARMY'

BACKGROUND

In 1935, 11 million Britons signed 'The Peace Ballot', a petition rejecting war. The mass slaughter and frightful consequences of the First World War had instilled a feeling that nothing was worth going through such hell for again.

The Treaty of Versailles, which ended the First World War, was also believed to have been extremely harsh on the defeated Germans. Most British politicians were accordingly prepared somehow to turn a blind eye to Hitler's takeover of German-speaking Austria, and even the German-speaking Sudetenland area of Czechoslovakia, which was accepted as a fait accompli by the Munich conference of September 1938.

By the end of the year Hitler had taken the rest of Czechoslovakia, and on 1 September 1939 he invaded Poland, while stories of his appalling mistreatment of Jews became more widespread. The scales finally fell from Britain's eyes and she declared war. In league with Stalin, Hitler quickly occupied Poland. Britain sent her army to France, who had also declared war and, for a while, very little happened – this was the 'Phony War'. Then the Germans unleashed Blitzkrieg. They invaded Denmark, Norway and then Belgium and Holland, before crossing the French border and cutting off the whole British army on the beaches of Dunkirk. Poised for the death blow, for some still unexplained reason, Hitler stayed his hand. Now, ordinary Englishmen, in their hopelessly inadequate 'pleasure craft', chugged and sailed off to Dunkirk and proceeded to rescue an army – and with it, eventually, the entire free world.

The evacuation of Dunkirk took place between 26 May and 4 June 1940.

On 14 May, when it was already obvious that Germany would surely be invading Britain, the British government broadcast a desperate message, pleading for recruits to join the 'Local Defence Volunteers'. Within a week, Churchill had changed the name to the 'Home Guard'. Others would call it 'Dad's Army'.

THE WEAPON

On 4 June 1940, in the House of Commons, Churchill summed up what was expected of the new force:

> ...WE SHALL DEFEND OUR ISLAND, WHATEVER THE COST MAY BE. WE SHALL FIGHT ON THE BEACHES, WE SHALL FIGHT ON THE LANDING GROUNDS, WE SHALL FIGHT IN THE FIELDS AND IN THE STREETS, WE SHALL FIGHT ON THE HILLS; WE SHALL NEVER SURRENDER.

In his appeal for potential recruits, one Home Guard colonel in Essex said, 'If you can walk and breathe, pull a trigger or pitch a bomb, your fellows are waiting – God bless you!'

By the end of June, one million men between the ages of 17 and 65 had signed up at the local police stations. The strength of the Home Guard remained above one million until they were 'stood down' towards the end of 1944.

But after the years of ignoring the threat of Germany and then the disaster of Dunkirk, where vast quantities of equipment had to be abandoned, Britain was hopelessly short of weapons.

The Home Guard were initially instructed to bring their own weapons: shotguns, pitchforks and even old pikes appear in photographs of those early parades. The uniforms were merely an armband and a cap. The recruits were either in 'reserved occupations', considered essential to the war effort, or too frail, old or young to join the regular army. No one doubted that invasion was imminent. It was the job of the Home Guard to slow down the highly trained, superbly equipped German army, until the regular British army could muster a counter-attack and throw the invaders back into the sea.

Initially the Home Guard was armed with anything that came to hand including pikes and pitchforks.

115

When effective weapons were issued, in December 1940, they were either relics of the First World War or shipped over from North America. The American P14 and P17 rifles looked alike, but one took .303-inch (7.7-mm) ammunition, the other .30-inch (7.6-mm) ammunition. Confusion was such that the P17 rifles were all painted with a red band.

WHAT HAPPENED

After the RAF won 'the battle of the skies' in the Battle of Britain, forcing Hitler to postpone and eventually abandon the invasion, the Home Guard continued to man anti-aircraft batteries, undertake guard and sentry duties and carry out bomb disposal work. In May 1941 and May 1943 they mounted guard at Buckingham Palace.

The Home Guard was disbanded in December 1944. By then 1,206 Home Guardsmen had lost their lives, two George Crosses and 13 George Medals had been won by Home Guardsmen, and Britain was safe.

THE STEN GUN

BACKGROUND

The Sten gun was a simple 9 mm submachine-gun created by the British in 1940 to meet the desperate demand for cheap and easily produced weaponry, in the face of almost certain invasion, after the catastrophic loss of equipment at Dunkirk. It was first issued to the British army in 1941.

THE WEAPON

The Sten was designed by Reginald Shepherd and Harold Turpin, and it took its name from the first letters of their surnames and the 'en' of Enfield, where the Small Arms Factory was situated.

The Mark III could be manufactured in only five man-hours, and the most basic versions consisted of only 47 parts. It was nicknamed the 'Woolworth Stench' or 'The Plumber's Nightmare' from its obvious cheapness and utilitarian, almost brutal, appearance. It was described as 'a pipe with a metal loop for a stock', and had a horizontal magazine – although the original Mark I did, in fact, have a wooden foregrip and handle.

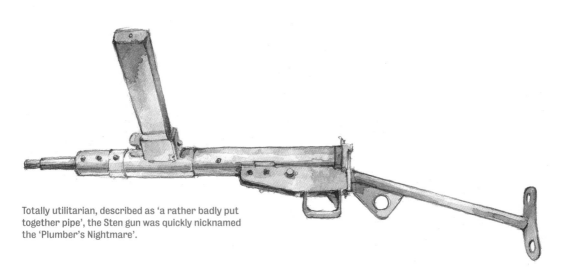

Totally utilitarian, described as 'a rather badly put together pipe', the Sten gun was quickly nicknamed the 'Plumber's Nightmare'.

The open-bolt, blowback-operated submachine-gun had a range of 50 yards (45 m) and could fire 500 rounds per minute from a 32-round detachable box magazine on the left. Single-shot or full automatic fire could be selected by a button above the trigger.

Four and a half million Stens were produced during the Second World War, half of which were Mark IIs. The attractions, to any wartime economy, of a lethal, reliable, weapon that was cheap and easy to produce were demonstrated when the Germans began manufacturing a copy, the MP3008, in 1945.

WHAT HAPPENED

The simplicity and size of the Sten meant that it was easy to disassemble, conceal and smuggle, as well as to repair and to copy. It was a favourite of guerrillas, resistance fighters, partisans, terrorists and citizen's armies throughout the world. Resistance groups in Norway, Denmark and Poland famously built Sten guns from scratch during the Second World War. Stens were used in the assassination of Reinhard Heydrich, Himmler's deputy and the effective head of the SS, in his open-topped car in Prague in May 1942 – an act which led to brutal reprisals in which two villages were completely destroyed and many thousands were killed.

Indira Gandhi, the Indian prime minister, was also assassinated with a Sten by her Sikh bodyguards in 1984.

The Sten remained in service with the British army until it was replaced by the Sterling submachine-gun in the 1960s. It continued to be used throughout the Commonwealth until the 1970s, and saw action in the 1971 war between India and Pakistan.

117

THE BREN GUN

BACKGROUND

The Bren gun was the main light machine gun used by British and Commonwealth infantry in the Second World War and saw combat with British forces for nearly 60 years up to and including the First Gulf War of 1991.

The name Bren comes from Bruno, the town in Czechoslovakia where it was designed, and Enfield, the site of the British Small Arms Factory, where it was produced from 1935.

THE WEAPON

Three classic features make the Bren instantly recognisable: the bipod, the conical flash hider at the end of the barrel, and the 30-round top box magazine with the trademark curve required to accommodate the rimmed, .303-inch (7.7.-mm) Lee Enfield rifle ammunition. The gas-operated Bren had air-cooled barrels, and each gun was issued with a spare so that barrels could be quickly changed if the gun overheated during sustained fire. Being magazine-fed, it had a slower rate of fire than belt-fed light machine guns, between 480 and 540 rounds per minute, but this also made it less prone to overheat and reduced the weight to almost 23 pounds (10.5 kg), enabling the Bren gunner to fire standing or on the move. The magazine also kept the ammunition clean, which reduced jamming. Effective range was 600 yards (550 m).

With its curved top-box magazine which takes the .303 Lee Enfield Rifle ammunition, the Bren gun is instantly recognisable.

It was originally envisaged that each 43-inch (1.09-m) long, 23-pound Bren would have a two-man crew: a gunner to fire and carry the Bren, and a reloader to carry ammunition and spare barrels, and to reload and change the barrels when in action. In practice, the weapon was normally operated by a single gunner in wartime.

The Bren was often mounted on tanks, armoured cars and other vehicles, especially Universal Carriers, which came to be known as Bren Gun Carriers. Anti-aircraft Brens took a 100-round drum magazine.

The Bren was simple, reliable and effective, veteran gunners claiming that any problems could be instantly cured by 'bashing it, turning the gauge, or both'.

WHAT HAPPENED

In 1958 the Bren was redesigned to accept the NATO 7.62 mm cartridges, with an almost straight magazine and new barrel. Though it remained in service with the British army until 1993, it was in due course largely superseded by the L7 General Purpose Machine Gun, a heavier belt-fed weapon, and then the L86 Light Support Weapon.

THE SPECIAL AIR SERVICE (SAS)

BACKGROUND

Britain's Special Air Service is the most admired special forces unit in the world. It evolved from the unit of volunteers who undertook raids behind enemy lines in the North African campaign of the Second World War in 1941.

THE WEAPON

It has seven main functions:

- Collecting intelligence in and around the battlefield
- Raiding and sabotage

- Counter-terrorism operations in the UK

- Counter-terrorism outside the UK

- Training allied conventional and unconventional 'forces'

- 'Counter revolutionary warfare activities' overseas

- VIP protection

The Special Air Service Regiment, with its famous 'Who Dares Wins' motto and cap badge, is a corps of the British army. It consists of one regular battalion-sized unit, 22 SAS Regiment, and two Territorial Army reserve units, 21 SAS Regiment and 23 SAS Regiment.

22 SAS Regiment has a number of operational 'sabre' squadrons divided into four specialised troops of 16 men each: the Air, Boat, Mobility and Mountain troops. The Air troops specialise in parachute infiltration. The Boat troops specialise in insertion via water, by helicopter, canoe, diving or submarine. The Mobility troops depend on vehicles to reach their area of operation, including fully armed and equipped Land Rovers, quad bikes and motorcycles. The Mountain troops are specially trained for cold weather and high-altitude operations.

Any male member of the British army who has already undertaken three years' service, is under 32, and has at least 39 months of service remaining, is allowed to apply for SAS 'Selection'. 'Selection' was introduced by Major John Woodhouse in 1952.

As many as 350 regular army soldiers apply to join the SAS every year. The SAS rarely

The SAS Mobility Troops customise landrovers, quad and motorbikes to suit the specific requirements of each engagement.

accepts more than nine. In order to be considered, they have to undergo the following selection procedure: 10 days of group orienteering and fitness training; 10 days of individual cross-country work; a 40-mile (64-km) march in 20 hours carrying a 55-pound (25-kg) rucksack; other physical tests, including a 4-mile (6.4-km) walk in under 30 minutes followed by swimming 2 miles (3.2 km) in under 90 minutes; one month of weapons training; one month of jungle training; a five-day evasion exercise in which candidates are tracked, caught and interrogated; courses in field medicine, signals, sniping, artillery spotting, demolitions, sabotage and languages.

After passing 'Selection', new recruits remain on probation for one year.

WHAT HAPPENED

In addition to their triumphs in North Africa, Italy, the Adriatic, the Middle East and Europe in the Second World War, the SAS has also won more recent battle honours in Malaysia, the Falklands, Sierra Leone, Iraq and Afghanistan. To the general public the SAS is perhaps best known for the spectacular rescue of hostages held at the Iranian Embassy in London in 1980, which was broadcast live on British television.

THE LANCASTER BOMBER

BACKGROUND

The Lancaster Bomber was the most successful night bomber of the Second World War, entering service with the RAF in early 1942 and dropping 608,612 tons of bombs in 156,000 sorties. It was the bomber that sank the Tirpitz and 'busted' the dams of the Ruhr valley.

THE WEAPON

The first prototype Lancaster flew on 9 January 1941 and was effectively a 'four-engined Manchester'. The earlier, twin-engined Manchester bomber was withdrawn from operations after only two years, in 1942, because of consistently unreliable engines. The Lancaster's four Rolls-Royce XX engines were to give no such troubles.

THE AVRO LANCASTER MK III

TYPE	Heavy bomber
CREW	7
POWER	Four 1,640 hp Rolls-Royce Merlin 28- or 38-cylinder V-type
SPEED	287 mph / 462 kph
FLIGHT HEIGHT	19,000 ft / 5,790 m
RANGE	1,730 miles / 2,784 km
WINGSPAN	102 ft / 31.09 m
LENGTH	69 ft 6 in / 21.18 m
WEIGHT	65,000 lb / 29,484 kg (loaded)
HEIGHT	20 ft 6 in / 6.26 m
NUMBER BUILT	7,377
IN SERVICE	1942–63
ARMAMENT	Two .303-in (7.7-mm) machine guns in nose turret, two .303-in (7.7-mm) machine guns in mid-upper (dorsal) turret, four more .303-in (7.7-mm) machine guns in tail turret, eight in all. Bomb load 22,000 lb / 10,000 kg max.

The Mark Ii Lancasters, of which 300 were built, were fitted with Bristol Hercules engines. The Mark IIIs, with Packard-built Merlin engines, were able to carry larger bombs, including the 21-foot, 12,000-pound Tallboys and, eventually, the 25½-foot, 22,000-pound Grand Slams.

On 20 August 1940, Winston Churchill said:

WE MUST NEVER FORGET THAT ALL THE TIME, NIGHT AFTER NIGHT, MONTH AFTER MONTH, OUR BOMBER SQUADRONS TRAVEL FAR INTO GERMANY, FIND THEIR TARGETS IN THE DARKNESS BY THE HIGHEST NAVIGATIONAL SKILL, AIM THEIR ATTACKS, OFTEN UNDER THE HEAVIEST FIRE, OFTEN WITH SERIOUS LOSS, WITH DELIBERATE CAREFUL

DISCRIMINATION, AND INFLICT SHATTERING BLOWS UPON THE WHOLE OF THE TECHNICAL AND WAR-MAKING STRUCTURE OF THE NAZI POWER.

To modern eyes the conditions in which the seven-man crew had to operate seem brutally basic. The bomb aimer spent most of his time lying on the floor at the front of the bomber, looking out of the transparent Perspex nose. When he needed to man his nose-turret twin Browning .303-inch (7.7-mm) guns, he simply stood up.

The pilot sat on top of the bomb bay, with his flight engineer beside him on a collapsible seat. Behind them were the navigator and wireless operator.

At the end of the bomb bay, in the dorsal turret, the mid-upper gunner had a 360-degree view over the top of the aircraft, using his two Browning .303 guns to defend the top and sides. The rear gunner, the 'tail-end Charlie', sat with his four Browning .303 guns over the spars of the tailplane. The mid-upper gunner and rear gunners had to wear electrically heated suits against the intense cold.

WHAT HAPPENED

Perhaps the most famous Lancaster bombing raid was 'Operation Chastise', in which No. 617 Squadron of the RAF dropped Barnes Wallis's famous bouncing bombs on three dams on the Eder River in Germany's industrial heartland – the Dam Busters Raid.

The dams provided vital hydroelectric power for the German war machine and water for the crucial German canal system. The Allies were also keen to persuade Stalin that they were making every effort to attack Germany on home soil and so divert Hitler's war effort away from the invasion of Russia.

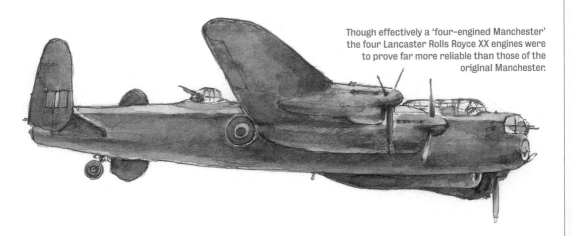

Though effectively a 'four-engined Manchester' the four Lancaster Rolls Royce XX engines were to prove far more reliable than those of the original Manchester.

Barnes Wallis was an aircraft designer by training who had designed the Wellesley and Wellington bombers. The obvious way to burst the three dams was with massive bombs dropped from a great height, but there were no aircraft then capable of carrying such a heavy load. Alternatively, if the bombs could be detonated in exactly the right place, much smaller charges could be used. Wallis had to find a way to deliver them. He eventually came up with the idea, based on the principle of a skimming stone, of bouncing the bomb on the water up to the dam wall and then running it down the wall to the dam's root. The bomb was code-named 'Upkeep'.

Avro Lancaster Mk IIIs were adapted to carry the drum-shaped bombs hanging below the aircraft. To lighten the Lancaster, the dorsal turret, bomb doors and most of the armour were removed.

The bombs had to be dropped at night, at 60 feet (18 m), at 240 mph (386 kph), and at exactly the right distance from the target. A special aiming device was devised for judging the distance, and angled spotlights, pointed downwards from the nose and fuselage, were used to judge the exact height. When the beams met on the surface of the water, the plane was at the correct height.

With incredible teamwork, self-sacrifice and determination, the 19 Lancasters and their 133 aircrew flew against all three dams, the Möhre, the Eder and the Sorpe. Two dams were breached and one was heavily damaged. Eight aircraft were lost, with 53 killed and three captured. Germany's loss of farm production, through flooding alone, did serious damage to German morale, while the photographs of the broken dams and flooding seriously boosted that of the Allies.

The aircrews won one Victoria Cross, five Distinguished Service Orders, ten Distinguished Flying Crosses and four bars, twelve Distinguished Flying Medals and two Conspicuous Gallantry Medals for the operation.

617 Squadron, which later dropped Wallis's vast Tallboy and Grand Slam bombs, still exists as a specialist unit, with the motto 'Après Moi le Déluge' (after me the flood).

A total of 7,374 Lancasters were built, of all variants, at an average cost of £47,000 each. Of these, 3,431 were lost in action in the Second World War. The fact that only 35 Lancasters managed to survive more than 100 operations illustrates the danger of crewing a Lancaster. The highest number of bombing raids undertaken by any single Lancaster was 139. In 1944 there were 42 Bomber Command Lancaster Squadrons. The last Lancaster raid of the war was made against a German SS barracks on 25 April 1945. The last Lancaster in military service was retired by the Royal Canadian Air Force in 1963.

Now, only 17 Lancasters remain.

THE CHURCHILL TANK and 'HOBART'S FUNNIES'

BACKGROUND

The Churchill was a heavily armoured British infantry tank, in service with the British army between 1941 and 1952, which was also adapted into a number of specialist vehicles, collectively known as 'Hobart's Funnies'.

It was named, appropriately, after Britain's great war prime minister of the Second World War, Winston Churchill, who had also played such an important role in the creation of the very first tank in the early years of the First World War.

THE WEAPON

Until Dunkirk and the surrender of France in 1940, British War Office tank design was directed towards coping with the needs of trench warfare like that of 1914–18. With France and Poland overrun, however, it was obvious that the new war would not mirror the last but instead would be much more mobile.

The original A20 trench tank design was speedily respecified into the A22. Most of Britain's armour had been abandoned at Dunkirk and, expecting invasion at any moment, the War Office demanded that the new Churchill A22 should begin production within 12 months. Accordingly, in June 1941, the almost untested Churchill Mk Is began to leave the factory.

The Churchill Tank could operate over ground inaccessible to other contemporary tanks. It also proved highly adaptable, providing the basis for Hobart's many 'funnies'.

The lack of testing showed. The engine was hard to reach, unreliable and under-powered, and the guns were too weak, but by March 1942 the Mark III was much improved, with a 6-pounder gun in a new turret. It proved highly effective in Africa and Italy.

By the Battle of Normandy in 1944, the even more effective Mark VII was in service, with its wider chassis, heavier armour and more powerful gun.

The great strength of the Churchill was its ability to negotiate terrain that was too difficult for all other tanks of the time. This was due to the eleven bogies on either side of the vehicle, each carrying two 10-inch wheels. Only nine of the bogies were weight-bearing, and the tank could retain mobility even after losing a number of wheels.

The Churchill also had thicker armour than all its adversaries, even the heaviest Germans. However, upgrades in guns and armour in the course of the war, and therefore weight, meant that, in the absence of engine upgrading, the speed declined in later models from 26 mph (42 kph) to 20 (32).

THE CHURCHILL TANK

PRODUCED	1941–5
IN SERVICE	1941–52
NUMBER BUILT	7,368
WEIGHT	38.5 tons
WIDTH	10 ft 8 in / 3 m
LENGTH	24 ft 5 in / 7.3 m
HEIGHT	8 ft 2 in / 2.8 m
CREW	5
ARMOUR	16–152 mm
SPEED	15 mph / 24 kph
ARMAMENT	Various including QF 2-pdr (0.91 kg) and QF 6-pdr (2.72 kg)
SECONDARY	2 x Besa machine guns

WHAT HAPPENED

A British specialism in the Second World War, and something at which they excelled, was the creation of 'specialist vehicles', tanks modified for very specific battlefield functions. The trigger was the necessity to breach the daunting beach defence system the Germans had constructed on the Channel coast of France between 1940 and 1942.

The British were convinced of the utility of specialist tank-based bridge layers, semi-aquatic recovery tanks to rescue flooded tanks on the shore, carpet layers to prepare reliable routes from the beaches, mine sweepers, charge layers and many others.

General Percy Hobart was the tank genius behind these innovations. He was passionate about tanks, and his 'flamboyant ideas' were such that he had been 'allowed to leave' the army in 1938. Churchill reinstated him. In 1942 he raised the 79th Armoured Division, trained it and led it into action in the invasion of Europe in 1944–5. He was specifically charged by Churchill with designing tank-based vehicles that might assist the D-Day landings in any way. He and his men came up with scores of designs, of which the following were perhaps the most effective.

The Churchill Tank Bridge could span 30 feet (9 m) and take a 40-ton load. The bridge was fitted where the turret would have been and pushed into place by hydraulics.

The Churchill Crocodile towed a fuel trailer which supplied a devastating flame-thrower fitted instead of the hull machinegun. This was copied by the Americans and proved highly effective on adapted Sherman tanks against the well dug-in Japanese on islands in the Pacific.

The AVREs, Assault Vehicle Royal Engineers, were Churchill tanks carrying demolition mortars, the 'Flying Dustbins', which pulverised concrete pillboxes. They were described as a 'godsend' on D-Day.

Flails carried vast chain flails on extended iron frameworks which whipped the ground well ahead of the tank, detonating the mines and clearing the path for others to follow.

The Duplex-Drivers, or DDs, were 'swimming tanks' with canvas screens that could be raised when necessary to give buoyancy, effectively turning the tank into a boat. Powered by propellers, the tanks 'swam' into the beaches ahead of the main battle force to provide protection for the following infantry.

THE SPECIAL OPERATIONS EXECUTIVE

BACKGROUND

After the evacuation of Dunkirk, before the Battle of Britain had even been joined, Hugh Dalton, the British Minister for Economic Warfare, recommended the creation of a 'new organisation to co-ordinate, inspire, control and assist the nationals of oppressed countries...'. Churchill agreed and sent Dalton a directive instructing him to 'set Europe ablaze'.

THE WEAPON

The new organisation was allocated an office, at 64 Baker Street, and a name: the Special Operations Executive, or SOE. Their job was to ferment resistance.

Recruits with in-depth knowledge and experience of the relevant enemy-occupied countries were given resistance training at Wanborough Manor, near Guildford, and then sent on commando courses in the Highlands. Stealth, sabotage, wireless telegraphy, armed and unarmed combat and particularly 'discreet assassination' were all covered.

The very existence of SOE caused outrage in some quarters. The British Chief of the Air Staff wrote:

> I THINK THE DROPPING OF MEN DRESSED IN CIVILIAN CLOTHES FOR THE PURPOSE OF ATTEMPTING TO KILL MEMBERS OF THE OPPOSING FORCES IS NOT AN OPERATION WITH WHICH THE ROYAL AIR FORCE SHOULD BE ASSOCIATED ... THERE IS A VAST DIFFERENCE, IN ETHICS, BETWEEN THE TIME HONOURED OPERATION OF DROPPING A SPY FROM THE AIR AND THIS ENTIRELY NEW SCHEME FOR DROPPING WHAT ONE CAN ONLY CALL ASSASSINS.

But it was not only men who would be dropped behind enemy lines. In April 1942, Churchill confirmed a directive that women too be infiltrated into Europe, 39 being sent to France alone. There was a real shortage of appropriately qualified recruits and the Gestapo were more likely to suspect a man, while women would be assumed to be going about perfectly innocent business.

SOE operatives were issued with a 2-foot (0.6 m) long, 30-pound (13.62-kg) short-wave Morse transceiver that needed 70 feet (21 m) of aerial to transmit and receive. The Germans could locate the position of any wireless in use within 30 minutes, so messages were brief, irregular and at differing wavelengths.

Every wireless operator was allocated different words that he or she was always to spell incorrectly. If the machine and codebook were captured and the Germans tried to continue transmitting, they would be detected immediately.

Part of the intense SOE training was guidance in how to withstand torture for two days – the time necessary for other agents to disappear in the event of a colleague's capture.

WHAT HAPPENED

SOE was particularly active in France, Belgium, Holland, Denmark, Poland and Yugoslavia. As head of her 'Wrestler Network' in France, Pearl Witherington organised over 1,500 Resistance fighters who obstructed the German army from inside France during the Allied D-Day landings. Francis Commarts's 'Jockey Network' of small self-sufficient cells included over 10,000 Resistance fighters.

Many hundreds of astoundingly brave men and women were involved with SOE, rescuing, harassing, sabotaging, assassinating and undermining the German war effort in any way possible. Two hundred lost their lives. General Eisenhower said of SOE:

IN NO OTHER WAR HAVE
RESISTANCE FORCES BEEN SO
CLOSELY HARNESSED TO THE
MAIN MILITARY EFFORT ... THEY
PLAYED A VERY CONSIDERABLE
PART IN OUR COMPLETE AND
FINAL VICTORY.

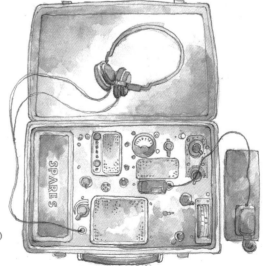

The cumbersome, suitcase-like, short-wave morse receiver with which every overseas SOE operative was issued required the deployment of 70 feet (21 m) of aerial before it could transmit and receive.

THE CENTURION TANK

BACKGROUND

In 1944 the War Office demanded a tank able to survive a direct hit from the German 88 mm anti-tank gun, and to compete with the Germans' bigger and better protected Panther and King Tiger tanks. It would be called the Centurion. Though it reached Europe before the end of the war in 1945, it was too late for actual combat.

THE WEAPON

Before the Centurion, tanks were divided into two classes and were known as 'infantry' and 'cruiser' tanks. The Centurion introduced the new class of all-purpose 'universal' or 'battle' tanks and has been described as 'one of the most successful tank designs of all time'.

The Centurion had 6-inch (152-mm) front armour and a 17-pound (7.72-kg) gun, a boat shaped, slope-fronted hull, wide tracks and a large turret. The size of earlier tanks had been restricted to allow them to be transported by rail, but in the Centurion the old limitations were abandoned.

THE CENTURION TANK			
IN SERVICE	1945–90s	**ARMOUR**	6 in / 152 mm
WEIGHT	51 tons	**SPEED**	21 mph / 34 kph
LENGTH	25 ft / 7.6 m	**POWER**	Rolls-Royce Meteor 650 hp
WIDTH	11 ft 1 in / 3.39 m	**ARMAMENT**	105 mm L7 rifled gun
HEIGHT	9 ft 10½ in / 3.01 m	**SECONDARY**	co-axial .30-in (7.6-mm)
CREW	4		Browning machine gun

The Rover-built Rolls-Royce Meteor engine, a variant of the superb Rolls-Royce Merlin aircraft engine, could generate speeds of over 21 mph (34 kph), and the exemplary design of the Centurion proved ideal for development, modification and upgrading.

Abandoning the old limitations that had been originally put in place to allow tanks to fit onto railway trucks, the Centurion Tank was one of the most successful tank designs of all time.

WHAT HAPPENED

In the Korean War of 1950–3 the terrain was not generally suitable for large-scale tank actions, but this was the first opportunity for the Centurion to prove itself in combat. The Mark III was an outstanding success in the smaller-scale battles, consistently outclassing the Chinese and Korean T-34/85s.

The Centurion Mk III's automatic stabilisation and control system allowed accurate fire while on the move, a major advance. This was later based on the use of a ranging machine gun which fired tracer as an aiming guide, and proved far more effective than the sophisticated optical and computerised controls used by the Americans. The introduction of the renowned 105 mm L7 rifled gun meant that the Centurion, in all its 13 different marks, was to remain in service with armies around the world until well into the 1990s.

THE BAe SEA HARRIER

BACKGROUND

The British Aerospace Sea Harrier FRS.1 evolved from the land-based Harrier GR1 and first took to the skies in 1978. One of the obvious differences from a traditional Harrier was the larger bubble cockpit, providing much better vision. It entered service on the Royal Navy's first 'vertical/short take-off and landing' carrier, HMS *Invincible*, in 1980.

In 1982 the military dictator of Argentina, General Galtieri, decided to claim and invade

The BAE Sea Harrier came into its own with the Task Force sent to liberate the Falkland Islands in 1982.

the British Falkland Islands in order to boost his popularity and divert attention away from his human rights abuses, corruption and economic mismanagement. The Falkland Islands have been British since 1765.

Galtieri assumed that no country could wage war on the other side of the world, and expected Britain to give up her citizens and territory without a fight. Instead Britain launched a 'Task Force' to rescue the islands.

THE WEAPON

The Sea Harriers of the Task Force were based on HMS *Hermes* and HMS *Invincible*, and fulfilled both air defence and ground attack roles. The aircraft-carriers were fitted with 'ski slopes' which allowed the Sea Harriers to take off with much more speed than with vertical take-off. The Argentinian aeroplanes were still faster, but by the time they reached the Task Force they only had five minutes before they had to return home, or risk running out of fuel. Not only were the Sea Harriers more manoeuvrable, they could stay in the air for 30 minutes and by working in shifts offered 24-hour protection to the carriers.

The Sea Harriers were armed with heat-seeking missiles, AIM-9L air-to-air sidewinders, with a speed of Mach 2.5 and an 80 per cent effectiveness record. They also had two 30 mm ADEN cannon, capable of firing 1,500 rounds a minute.

They won 22 air-to-air engagements, losing none of their own, although two were lost to ground fire. On 21 May, at the height of hostilities, pairs of Harriers were leaving on combat patrol every 20 minutes.

THE BAe SEA HARRIER FA2

TYPE	Combat aircraft
CREW	1
POWER	One 21,500-lb (9,760 kg) thrust Rolls-Royce Pegasus MK 106 vectored thrust turbofan
SPEED	736 mph / 1,185 kph
FLIGHT HEIGHT	51,000 ft / 15,545 m
RANGE	115 miles / 185 km
WINGSPAN	25 ft 3 in / 7.70 m
LENGTH	46 ft 6 in / 14.17 m
WEIGHT	26,200 lb / 11,880 kg (loaded)
HEIGHT	12 ft 2 in / 3.71 m
NUMBER BUILT	57
IN SERVICE	1993–2006
ARMAMENT	Two 1-in Aden cannon; five external pylons for AIM-9L sidewinder, AIM-120 AMRAAM; two Harpoon or Sea Eagle anti-ship missiles, up to 8,000 lb / 3,630 kg total

WHAT HAPPENED

In 1988 the Sea Harrier was upgraded to allow a larger air-to-air weapons load, look down radar, a longer range and an enhanced cockpit display: requirements highlighted by active service in the Falklands War. Delivered in 1993, the upgraded Sea Harrier was known as the FA2.

The Royal Navy retired the Sea Harrier in 2006. It has not been replaced.

133

THE AVRO VULCAN

BACKGROUND

The Avro Vulcan was the world's first 'delta wing' bomber. It carried Britain's first nuclear weapon and set a new record for the world's longest bombing raid. It served with the RAF from 1956 to 1984.

THE WEAPON

The Vulcan was originally intended to fulfil a nuclear role, but this was relinquished to the Royal Navy's Polaris submarines in 1970. It was designed to carry 21 1,000-pound (454 kg) bombs and was involved in conventional combat during the Falklands War of 1982.

The distance between the Ascension Islands and the Falklands is 3,380 nautical miles. Each mission consumed 1.1 million gallons of fuel and required air-to-air refuelling by Victor aircraft. In only three weeks, in April 1982, British engineers were able to modify the craft to make this possible and achieve raids over the longest distances ever attempted. The runway at Stanley on the occupied Falkland Islands was cut on the first raid.

Despite its size the Vulcan had a relatively small radar cross-section. Through sheer accident, the designers had hit on the new 'stealth' profile. The Vulcan B2 variant entered service in 1960. It had a larger wing with a different leading edge and a distinctive kink to reduce turbulence. This provided much better performance.

In producing the first delta wing bomber the designers of the Avro Vulcan had accidentally hit upon the first Stealth profile.

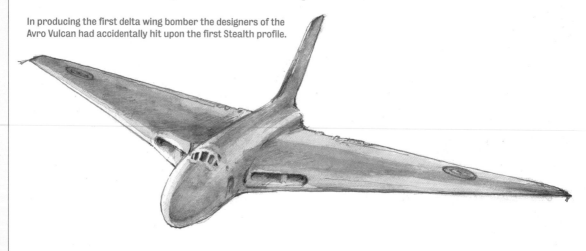

THE AVRO VULCAN B.2

TYPE	Strategic bomber
CREW	5
POWER	Four 20,000-lb (9.072-kg) thrust Bristol Siddeley Olympus MK.301 turbojets
SPEED	645 mph / 1,038 kph
FLIGHT HEIGHT	65,000 ft / 19,810 m
RANGE	4,600 miles / 7,403 km
WINGSPAN	111 ft / 33.83 m
LENGTH	99 ft 11 in / 30.45 m
WEIGHT	250,000 lb / 113,398 kg (loaded)
HEIGHT	27 ft 2 in / 8.28 m
NUMBER BUILT	136
IN SERVICE	1956–84
ARMAMENT	21 x 1,000 lb high-explosive bombs Yellow sun MK.2 or WE.177 B nuclear weapons Blue Steel ASM with Red Snow nuclear warhead

WHAT HAPPENED

After the Falklands six Vulcan B2s were converted into air-to-air refuelling tankers and served with 50 Squadron for two years until 1984.

Of the 136 Vulcans built, only one remains in working order.

PART V

MEDALS

THE VICTORIA CROSS (VC)

The highest military award for conspicuous bravery in the presence of the enemy. Instituted by Queen Victoria in 1856, the VC consists of a bronze Maltese cross and the royal crown, with a lion in the centre, under which are the words 'For Valour'. The ribbon is claret-coloured. Worn on the left breast, it takes precedence over all other decorations.

Until 1942, the VC was manufactured from the metal of guns captured at Sebastopol in the Crimean War. To date, 1,355 have been awarded.

THE GEORGE CROSS (GC)

The highest civilian award 'for acts of the greatest heroism or of the most conspicuous courage in circumstances of extreme danger', the GC is only awarded to service personnel for acts of heroism not covered by military honours.

Instituted in 1940, the GC consists of a silver cross with St George and the Dragon in the centre. The words 'For Gallantry' encircle St George and the Dragon. It hangs from a dark blue ribbon.

The GC has been awarded to 156 people, 84 posthumously. The island of Malta, in 1942, and the Royal Ulster Constabulary, in 1999, were awarded the decoration collectively.

THE BANNERET

Last properly conferred by Charles I in 1642 on Colonel John Smith for his recapture of the Royal Standard at the battle of Edgehill, this order of Knighthood was conferred on the field of battle for acts of exceptional gallantry by tearing off the points of the recipient's pennant (the banner under which the captain had lead his vassals into battle).

ORDER OF THE BRITISH EMPIRE

Instituted by George V in 1917, the award honours those who have rendered service to the United Kingdom and its people and is split into Military and Civil Divisions. There

are now over 100,000 living members of the order in Britain and abroad. From its very inception the order included women and foreigners who had contributed to the British war effort. The motto of the order is 'For God and the Empire'.

The order consists of five classes:

- Knights (or Dames) Grand Cross in the Most Excellent Order of the British Empire (GBE)

- Knights (or Dames) in the Most Excellent Order of the British Empire (KBE)

- Commander of the Most Excellent Order of the British Empire (CBE)

- Officer in the Most Excellent Order of the British Empire (OBE)

- Member of the Most Excellent Order of the British Empire (MBE)

ORDER OF THE COMPANIONS OF HONOUR

Instituted in 1917 by George V, the order is conferred on men and women for services of national importance. The order consists of the Sovereign and 65 ordinary members. The motto of the order is 'In action faithful and in honour clear'.

DISTINGUISHED SERVICE ORDER (DSO)

Instituted by Queen Victoria in 1886, the order is awarded for meritorious or distinguished services by members of the armed forces of the rank of major (or its equivalent) or above during wartime. (The DSO is very occasionally awarded to more junior officers for especially gallant actions.)

The medal's official description runs: 'Gold cross, enamelled white, edged gold, having on one side thereof in the centre, within a wreath of laurel enamelled green, the Imperial Crown in gold upon a red enamelled ground and on the reverse, within a similar wreath on a similar red ground, Our Imperial and Royal cipher, VRI, shall be suspended from the left breast by a red riband, edged blue, of one inch in width.'

CONSPICUOUS GALLANTRY CROSS (CGC)

Instituted in 1995 by Queen Elizabeth II, the CGC is awarded for conspicuous gallantry in action, performed by all ranks of the armed services. The ribbon is white with a red central stripe and blue edges.

DISTINGUISHED SERVICE CROSS (DSC)

Instituted by King Edward VII in 1901 (as the Conspicuous Service Cross), the DSC is awarded for gallant or distinguished naval service in the face of the enemy. The ribbon is blue with a white central stripe.

MILITARY CROSS (MC)

Instituted by King George V in 1914, the MC is awarded for gallant and distinguished services in action. The ribbon is white with a purple central stripe.

DISTINGUISED FLYING CROSS (DFC)

Instituted by King George V in 1918, the DFC is awarded for courage or devotion to duty while flying in active service against the enemy. The ribbon is white with diagonal purple stripes.

AIR FORCE CROSS (AFC)

Instituted by King George V in 1918, the AFC is awarded for courage or devotion to duty while flying. The ribbon is white with diagonal red stripes.

CONSPICUOUS GALLANTRY MEDAL (CGM)

Instituted in 1855 (for the Crimean War only) and reinstituted in 1874, it was replaced by the Conspicuous Gallantry Cross in 1993. The CGM is awarded to other ranks in the Royal Navy, Royal Marines or merchant navy for acts of gallantry in action. The ribbon is white with dark blue edges.

THE GEORGE MEDAL (GM)

Instituted in 1940, the GM is awarded for outstanding acts of bravery that nevertheless do not qualify for the George Cross. A round medal, with St George and the Dragon on one side and the head of the Sovereign on the reverse, it hangs from a red ribbon with five narrow blue stripes.

DISTINGUISHED SERVICE MEDAL (DSM)

Instituted in 1914, the DSM is awarded to other ranks of the Royal Navy or Royal Marines for distinguished conduct in the face of the enemy. The ribbon is blue with a double white central stripe.

MILITARY MEDAL (MM)

Instituted in 1916, the MM is awarded to other ranks of the army and Royal Air Force for acts of bravery in the field. The blue ribbon has a white central stripe bearing two red stripes.

DISTINGUISHED FLYING MEDAL (DFM)

Instituted in 1918, the DFM is awarded to other ranks of the Royal Air Force for acts of bravery while flying in the face of the enemy. The ribbon is white with narrow diagonal purple stripes.

AIR FORCE MEDAL (AFM)

The AFM is awarded to other ranks of the Royal Air Force for courage or devotion to duty in the air. The ribbon is white with narrow diagonal red stripes.